WARRIORS
The GREATEST Fighters in History

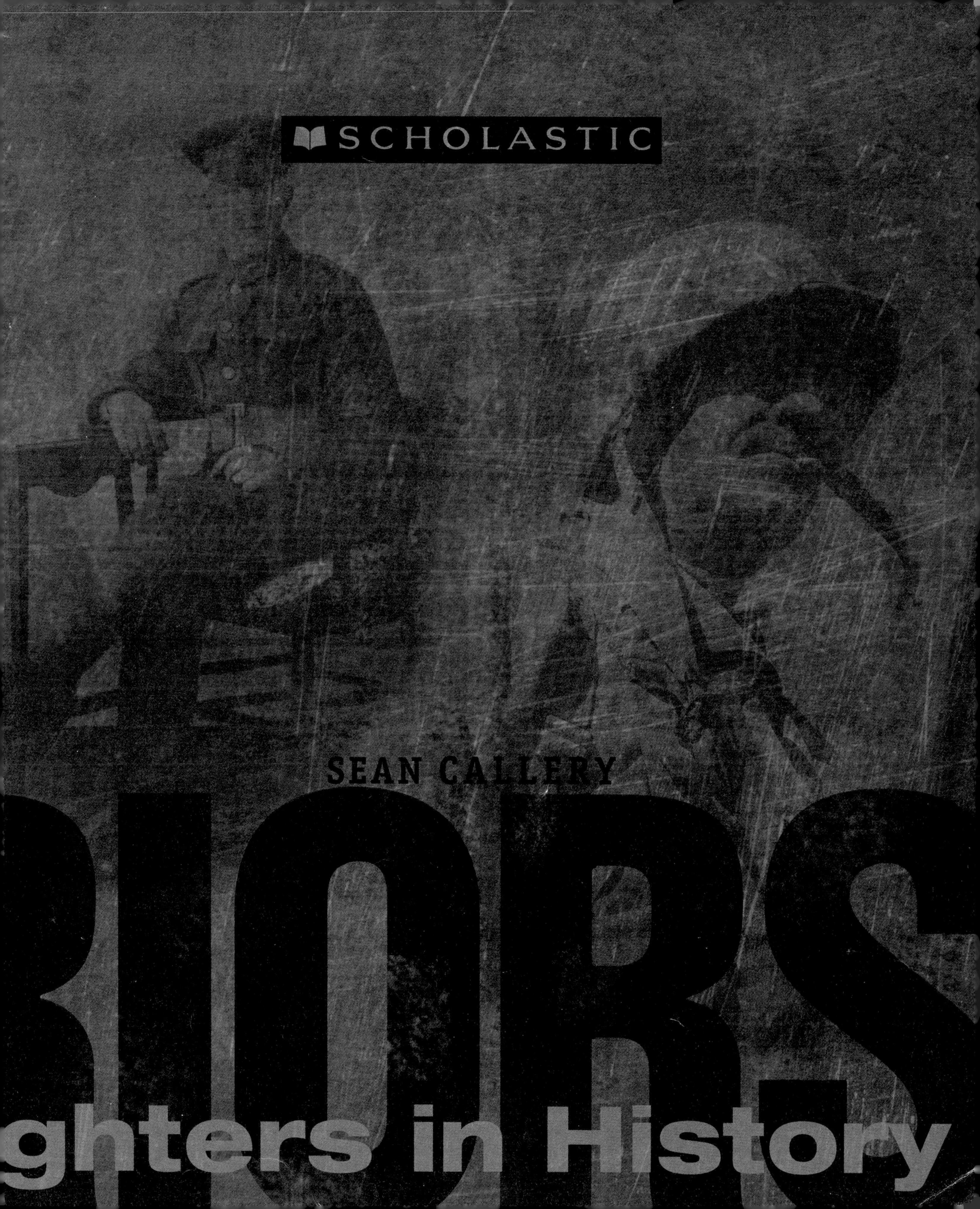

SEAN CALLERY

RIORS

ghters in History

■■SCHOLASTIC

Art director: Bryn Walls
Managing editor: Miranda Smith
Consultant: Tony Watts, Armorer, Bapty & Co.
Special photography taken at Bapty & Co.
by Gary Ombler

ISBN 978-0-545-85184-8

10 9 8 7 6 5 4 3 2 1   15 16 17 18 19

Printed in the U.S.A.   08
First printing, September 2015

contents

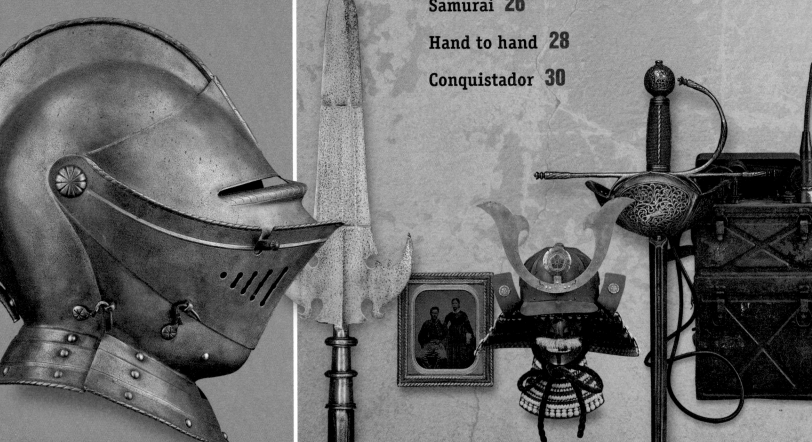

foreword

For thousands of years, people have fought battles to defend their homes, their rulers, and their countries; for personal honor; or to gain glory, riches, or territory. And legendary warriors and heroes have emerged from among the ranks of soldiers on the battlefield.

In this book, you will meet the toughest of these warriors—from ancient Greek hoplites and Roman legionaries to medieval knights and samurai to modern Navy SEALs and desert troops. And they all have something in common: They are highly effective because they train their whole lives, honing their bodies and their skills with weapons to perfection.

Ancient armor
The overlapping body armor of the Roman legionary was heavy and hot to wear, but it gave protection against the enemy sword or javelin.

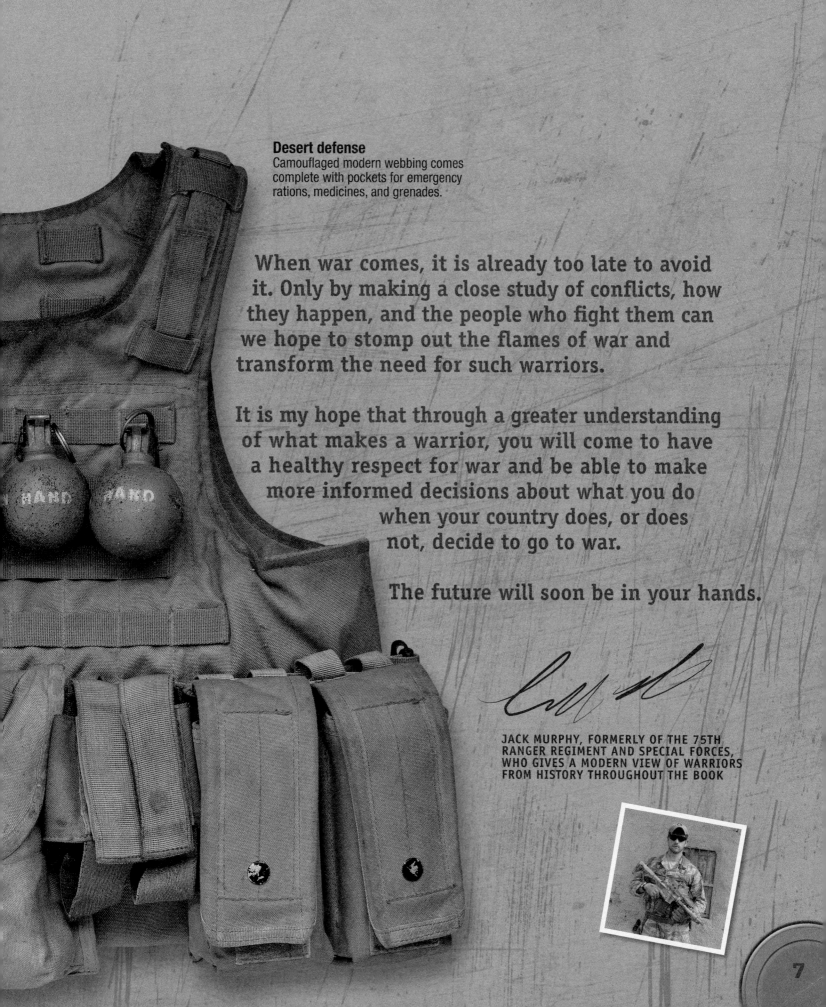

Desert defense
Camouflaged modern webbing comes complete with pockets for emergency rations, medicines, and grenades.

When war comes, it is already too late to avoid it. Only by making a close study of conflicts, how they happen, and the people who fight them can we hope to stomp out the flames of war and transform the need for such warriors.

It is my hope that through a greater understanding of what makes a warrior, you will come to have a healthy respect for war and be able to make more informed decisions about what you do when your country does, or does not, decide to go to war.

The future will soon be in your hands.

JACK MURPHY, FORMERLY OF THE 75TH RANGER REGIMENT AND SPECIAL FORCES, WHO GIVES A MODERN VIEW OF WARRIORS FROM HISTORY THROUGHOUT THE BOOK

Dory (long spear)
This 10-foot-long (3 m) spear was a hoplite's main weapon. Soldiers advanced in a group, protected by their shields, stabbing their blades into gaps in the enemy's defenses.

Metal casing
Helmets offered protection but made hearing difficult, so orders given in battle were short and sharp.

CORINTHIAN BRONZE HELMET

HOPLITE

HOPLITE, A HEAVILY ARMED INFANTRYMAN

Rows of Greek hoplites sang to their gods as they pushed forward to crash against enemy shields. They were a fighting team, thrusting out their long, sharp spears as they jogged behind a wall of shields, each man protecting those next to him. This close arrangement of soldiers, called a phalanx, was almost unstoppable.

Easy to spot
Brightly colored horsehair plumes on the helmets of commanders made them look bigger and more fearsome.

ARMOR
Hard fighting
It was very hot inside the heavy bronze armor, and difficult to see clearly. If a man fell, he was often trampled as he tried to get up.

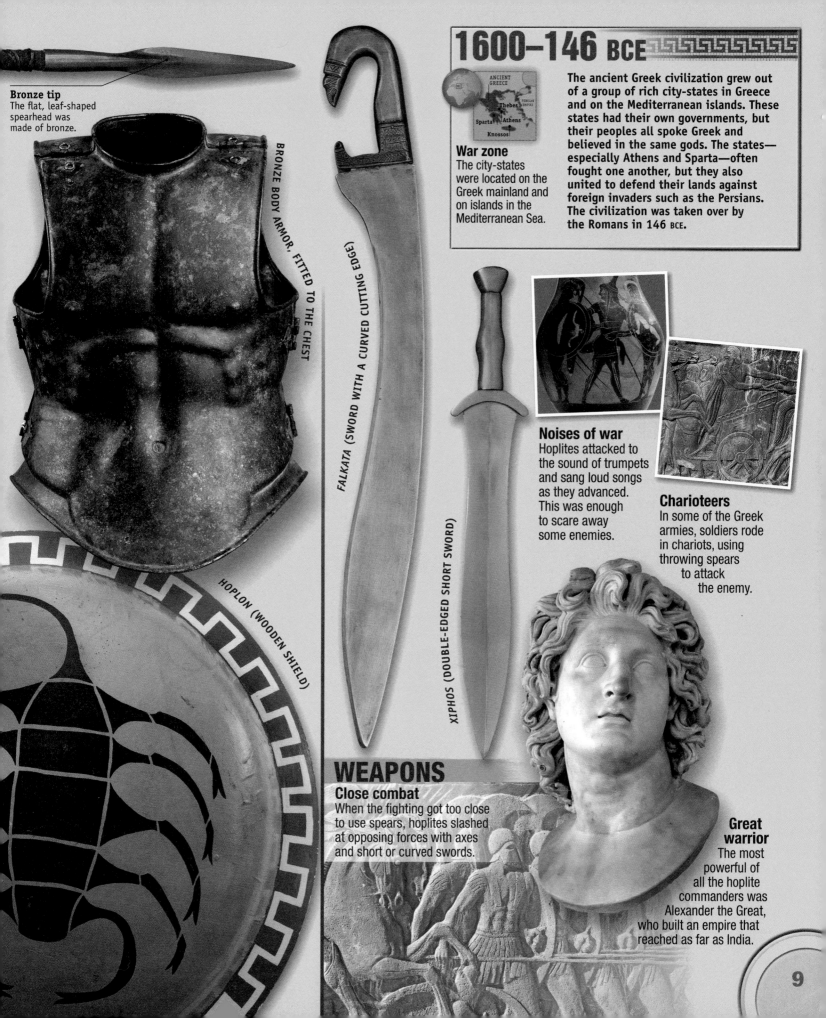

Bronze tip
The flat, leaf-shaped spearhead was made of bronze.

BRONZE BODY ARMOR. FITTED TO THE CHEST

FALKATA (SWORD WITH A CURVED CUTTING EDGE)

HOPLON (WOODEN SHIELD)

XIPHOS (DOUBLE-EDGED SHORT SWORD)

The ancient Greek civilization grew out of a group of rich city-states in Greece and on the Mediterranean islands. These states had their own governments, but their peoples all spoke Greek and believed in the same gods. The states—especially Athens and Sparta—often fought one another, but they also united to defend their lands against foreign invaders such as the Persians. The civilization was taken over by the Romans in 146 BCE.

War zone
The city-states were located on the Greek mainland and on islands in the Mediterranean Sea.

Noises of war
Hoplites attacked to the sound of trumpets and sang loud songs as they advanced. This was enough to scare away some enemies.

Charioteers
In some of the Greek armies, soldiers rode in chariots, using throwing spears to attack the enemy.

WEAPONS

Close combat
When the fighting got too close to use spears, hoplites slashed at opposing forces with axes and short or curved swords.

Great warrior
The most powerful of all the hoplite commanders was Alexander the Great, who built an empire that reached as far as India.

9

To the point
An advancing legionary threw his 6.5-foot-long (2 m) pilum (javelin) at the enemy from a distance of 15 m (50 feet). Then he charged.

Handhold
Cord was wrapped around the shaft to make a handle.

Lead weight
This was added for balance.

LEGIONARY

ROMAN LEGIONARY

The Roman army was a killing machine. Its soldiers were full-time professionals, serving their masters for up to 25 years. Well equipped, in good shape, and very well trained, these men helped build one of the greatest empires in history.

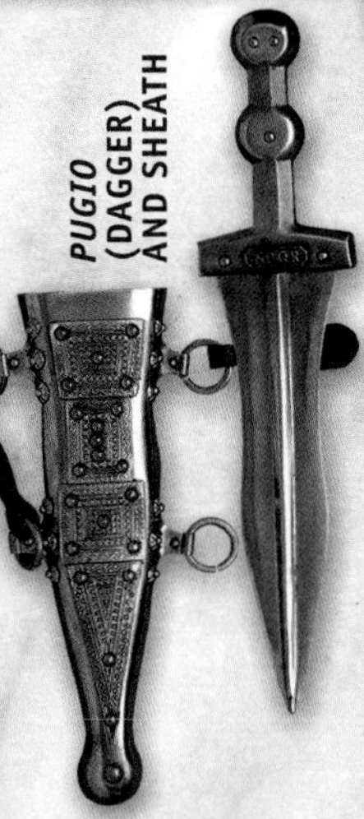

PUGIO (DAGGER) AND SHEATH

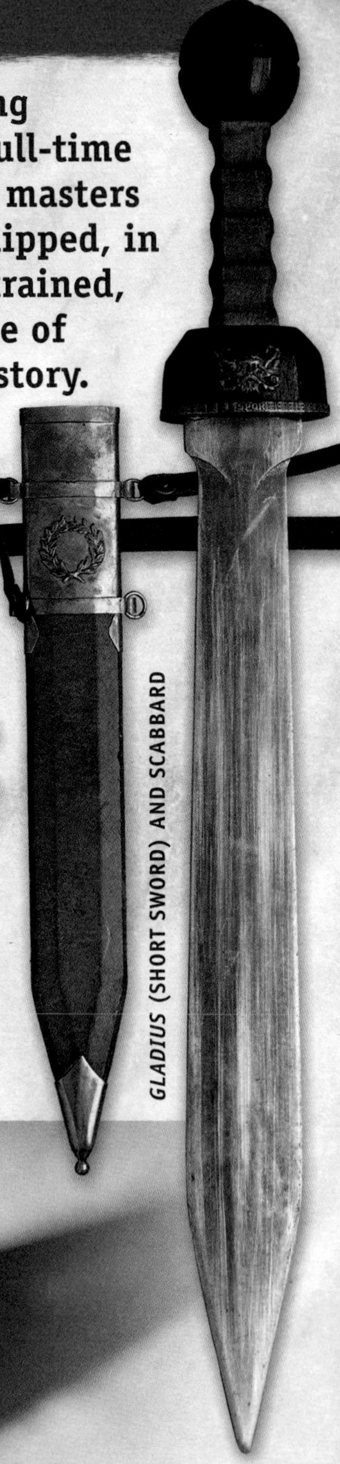

GLADIUS (SHORT SWORD) AND SCABBARD

Siege weapon
This giant catapult fired rocks over defensive walls during a siege.

WEAPONS
Fully armed
A legionary carried two javelins, a shield, a sword, and a dagger. His sword was the ideal length for stabbing the enemy in the stomach in close combat.

LORICA SEGMENTATA (TORSO ARMOR)

No reuse
The iron shank bent or broke on impact, so it could not be thrown back.

ROMAN EMPIRE

Rome

Ruling all
Generals such as Julius Caesar built an empire with unmatched military power.

The Roman Empire was based in Italy, but at one time it stretched across much of Europe, east into Asia, and south into North Africa. At its height, one in every four people on Earth lived under Roman rule. From 58 BCE, in a series of military campaigns, the famous Roman general Julius Caesar conquered the Celts in Gaul and Britain.

Roman general Julius Caesar

Celt

The Romans defeated the Celts to take over western Europe. Celtic warriors roared as they ran into battle. They fought with spears and broad swords, but had little armor.

CELTIC WOOD AND BRONZE SHIELD

DOUBLE-EDGED SWORD

GALEA (HELMET)

Cheek guard
The large, hinged cheekpieces protected the face.

SPEAR

CELTIC TRIBESMAN

Shield wall
The Romans used a tortoise formation—a group of soldiers held shields above their heads and at their sides. This protected them from flying arrows.

ARMOR

Battle tactics
Armored troops marched toward the enemy in lines four rows deep. They left space between them to swing their swords.

CURVED SCUTUM (SHIELD)

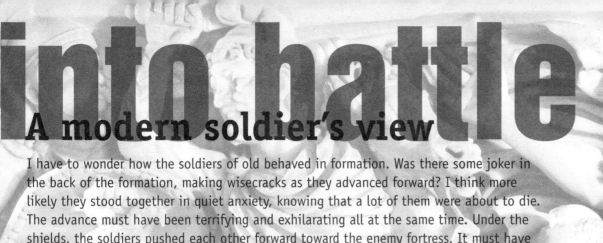

into battle

A modern soldier's view

I have to wonder how the soldiers of old behaved in formation. Was there some joker in the back of the formation, making wisecracks as they advanced forward? I think more likely they stood together in quiet anxiety, knowing that a lot of them were about to die. The advance must have been terrifying and exhilarating all at the same time. Under the shields, the soldiers pushed each other forward toward the enemy fortress. It must have gotten hot and sweaty—not to mention frightening, as your fellow soldiers were brought down around you. At the same time, you functioned as a military machine, a human siege weapon. But I have my doubts that the rank and file in the Roman army were overly enthusiastic about camping out and fighting barbarians for years on end.

—JACK MURPHY, FORMERLY OF THE 75TH RANGER REGIMENT AND SPECIAL FORCES

In the thick of it
This carving from a Roman tomb shows legionaries fighting "barbarians"—the term that Romans used to describe people who lived outside the Roman Empire.

13

Roman soldier **AMMIANUS MARCELLINUS** tells the story of the Battle of Adrianople, in modern Turkey, on August 9, 378 CE. The Romans were battling to save their empire from the Goths of northern Europe.

After an 8-mile march, we arrived at noon and saw the circle of wagons of the enemy army. The Goths let out fierce yells and set fire to the fields all around, so neither we nor our horses could eat the crops.

Then they descended from the mountains like a thunderbolt, spreading confusion and slaughter among all they came across on their rapid charge.

Our men began to retreat; but the officers yelled fresh orders and they made a fresh stand. The soldiers were terrified, and many were pierced by strokes from the javelins and arrows hurled at them.

The two lines of battle dashed against each other like warships, and, thrusting with all their might, were tossed to and fro like the waves of the sea. Our left wing managed to advance up to the Goths' wagons, but the rest of the cavalry didn't support them, and they were beaten back down.

Now our infantry was left stranded, huddling so close together that a soldier could hardly draw his sword. In the clouds of dust, we could hardly

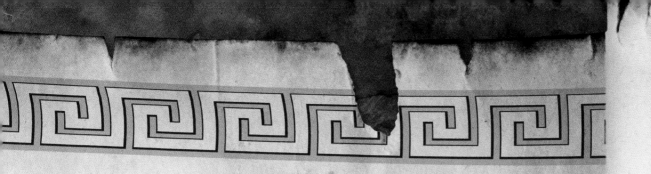

SEE THE SKY, SO WE DIDN'T EVEN SEE THE ARROWS THAT LANDED WITH DEADLY RESULTS.

THE GOTHS RUSHED IN AND BEAT DOWN OUR HORSES AND MEN, AND LEFT NOWHERE FOR OUR RANKS TO FALL BACK. WE WERE SO CLOSELY PACKED THAT IT WAS HARD TO MOVE. OUR MEN AGAIN TOOK UP THEIR SWORDS AND SLEW ALL THEY ENCOUNTERED, AND AS WE EXCHANGED BLOWS, HELMETS AND BREASTPLATES WERE DASHED TO PIECES.

THE PLAIN WAS COVERED WITH BODIES, AND THE AIR FILLED WITH THE GROANS OF THE DYING, OR OF MEN FEARFULLY WOUNDED. IN ALL THIS CONFUSION, OUR INFANTRY.MEN WERE EXHAUSTED. THEY HAD NEITHER STRENGTH LEFT TO FIGHT, NOR SPIRITS TO PLAN ANYTHING. THEIR SPEARS WERE BROKEN BY THE FREQUENT COLLISIONS. KNOWING THAT ESCAPE WAS IMPOSSIBLE, THEY THRUST THEIR SWORDS INTO THE DENSE BATTALIONS OF THE ENEMY.

OUR FORCES FLED AS EACH MAN TRIED TO SAVE HIMSELF AS WELL AS HE COULD. THE GOTHS FOLLOWED. THEY SPARED NEITHER THOSE WHO SURRENDERED NOR THOSE WHO CARRIED ON FIGHTING. HALF-DEAD MEN BLOCKED THE ROADS, MOANING WITH THE PAIN OF THEIR WOUNDS. HEAPS OF DEAD HORSES PILED UP.

AT LAST A DARK, MOONLESS NIGHT PUT AN END TO THE TERRIBLE DISASTER.

DOUBLE-EDGED SWORD

Sword with a name
A warrior's sword was probably the most expensive item he owned. Many swords were given names, such as "Leg-biter," and passed from father to son.

Less metal
A groove down the length of the steel blade made the sword less heavy, and easier to smash down on an enemy's shield.

VIKING

VIKING SWORDSMAN

Vikings were the ultimate smash-and-grab raiders. Sailing in small fleets, they targeted a settlement, attacked, and then got away before defenders could get organized. They stole treasures and terrified everyone. These warriors were young, eager for glory—and prepared to fight to the death.

DRAGON FIGUREHEAD

LONGSHIP IN FULL SAIL

Leather armor
Some wealthier warriors wore leather for protection in battle. They hardened the leather with melted beeswax.

Scramasax
The Viking dagger was single edged and used as both a tool and a weapon.

DAGGER AND SHEATH

STAGES OF BUILDING A LONGSHIP

TRANSPORT

Longships
These "dragon ships," built of overlapping planks, were sturdy enough for the open ocean but could also sail up shallow rivers.

WEAPONS AND

Battle tactics
The Vikings began their attacks behind a wall of shields, thrusting at the enemy with axes and spears. Then they moved forward, swinging their swords.

PLAITED LEATHER ARMOR

YEW-WOOD BOW AND ARROW

Feathered flight
Feathers, such as these from a goose, were balanced to help the arrow fly straight.

793–1066

The New World
In 1001, Leif Eriksson was the first European to land in North America.

The Vikings came from Norway, Denmark, and Sweden. Their first raids were on the British Isles, but eventually they raided and traded over huge distances, sailing east as far as Russia. They also traveled west across the Atlantic, reaching Newfoundland, Canada, via Iceland and Greenland.

Viking explorer Leif Eriksson

IRON HELMET AND MAIL NECK SHIELD

BATTLE-AX

THROWING AX

WOOD AND LEATHER BATTLE SHIELD

Anglo-Saxon

Britain was ruled by Anglo-Saxon chieftains. They built fortified towns to protect their kingdoms from one another and from the Viking raiders who terrorized their shores.

SHIELD WITH AN EAGLE, SYMBOL OF FEARLESSNESS

DAGGER AND SCABBARD

FIGHTING AX

Aventail
This flexible curtain of mail attached to the helmet protected the throat, neck, and shoulders.

Ax power
Thrown with deadly accuracy, the Viking ax could split a man's head in two.

ANGLO-SAXON SOLDIER

Defensive shield
Made of wooden planks, this was made to measure and covered with leather or cloth. The warrior gripped a handle across the center of the back.

ARMOR

VIKING GODS

Gods and men
Viking warriors were inspired by their gods. Their ambition was to die in combat and travel to Valhalla, the hall of the gods, in Asgard. Thor, the hammer-wielding god of thunder, was their ideal. Today, Thor has become a comic-book superhero who features in popular action films.

BRONZE STATUE OF THOR (CA. 1000), FOUND IN ICELAND

CHRIS HEMSWORTH AS THOR IN THE FILM *THOR* (2011)

17

SHIELDS

For more than 2,000 years, the shield was a vital piece of military equipment. Warriors used shields of all shapes and sizes to block flying arrows and deflect blows from axes, maces, and slashing swords.

Viking, ca. 900
This large wooden shield was gripped in the center from behind an iron boss to protect the warrior's hand.

Indian *dhal*, 1600s
The warrior held this steel shield firmly by putting his arm through two handles on the back.

Italian, 1500s
Many Italian shields of this period are richly decorated, taking their inspiration from battle scenes of ancient Rome.

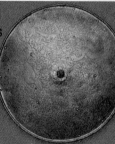

French, 1500s
Armorers used acid to etch patterns into shields that would not weaken the metal for battle.

Bontok, 1600s
The shields of the head-hunting Bontok of the Philippines are 3 feet (1 m) long. The men cut them from single pieces of wood.

Mughal *sipar*, 1700s
This decorated shield is made of iron and steel. The most prized Mughal shields were made of rhinoceros hide.

Beja, Sudan
This African shield is made of elephant hide. It has a high-domed central boss to protect the warrior's hand.

Masai, Kenya
Made of cattle hide, each Masai shield is decorated differently. Only older warriors are allowed to use the color red.

<< Iron Age, 350–50 BCE
The red glass studs on this bronze shield would have shone brightly in sunlight and startled an enemy.

< Ethiopian, 1800s
In Ethiopia, shields were small but highly decorated. A warrior rarely wore armor but usually had a shield.

Cut and thrust
The arming sword was in common use from 1000 to 1350. The long sword then became the weapon of choice.

SINGLE-HANDED ARMING SWORD

HAND-AND-A-HALF LONG SWORD

MOUNTED KNIGHT

MEDIEVAL KNIGHT

An armored knight thundering toward you on horseback must have looked like a metal-coated superhero whom no weapon could harm. If he did not strike you with his long lance, he would dismount to hack at you with his sharp sword. Knights honed their fighting skills in mock battles called jousts.

WOODEN SHIELD DECORATED WITH THREE LIONS PASSANT

ONE-HANDED FLAIL

WAR HAMMER

MACE

CROSSBOW BOLT

CROSSBOW

WEAPONS
Attack force
From horseback, different weapons could be wielded with great effect—in particular the mace and the lance, the favorite weapons of many knights.

Crossbow
This could fire a sharpened metal bolt with enough force to cut through armor.

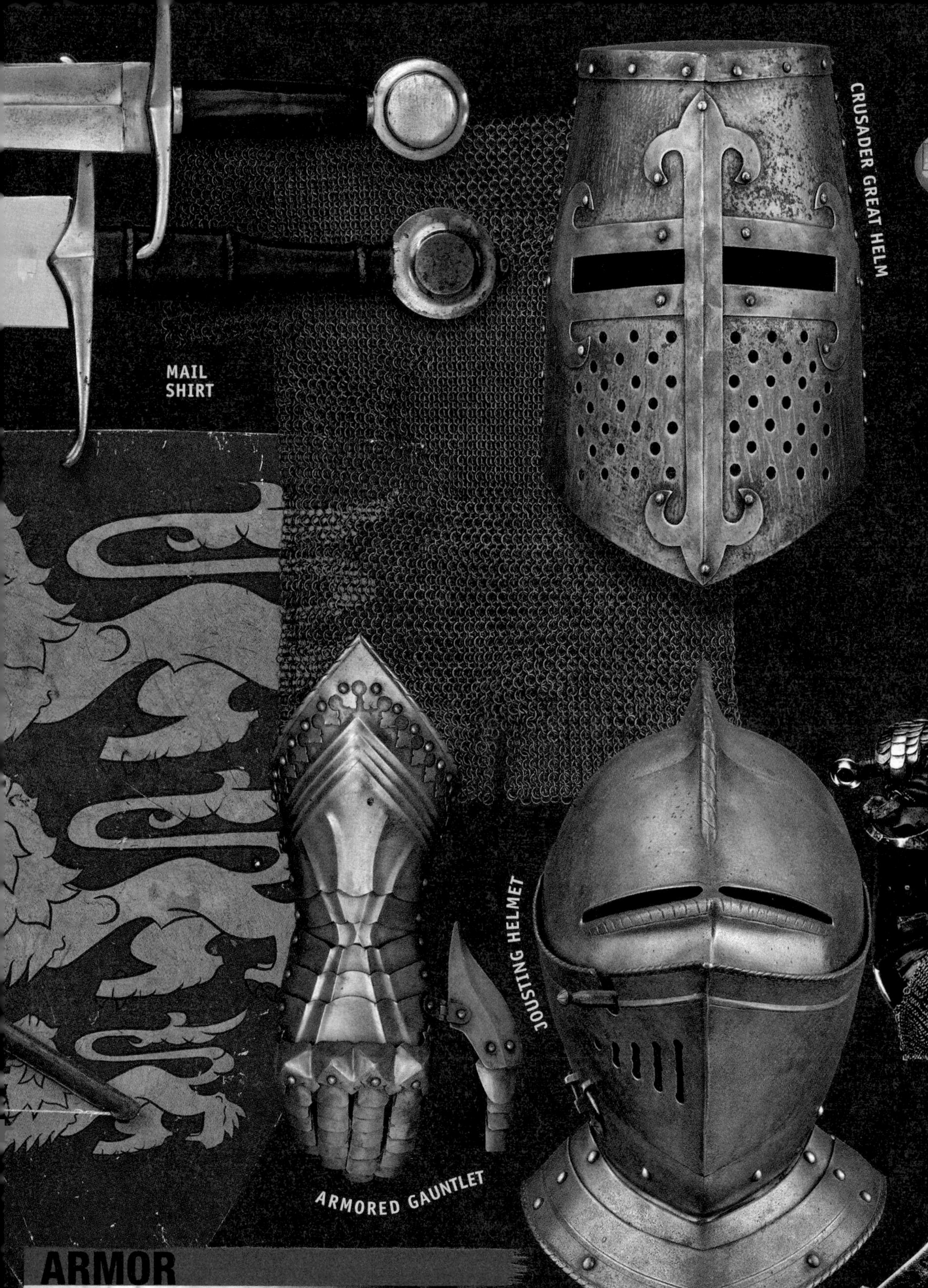

MAIL SHIRT

CRUSADER GREAT HELM

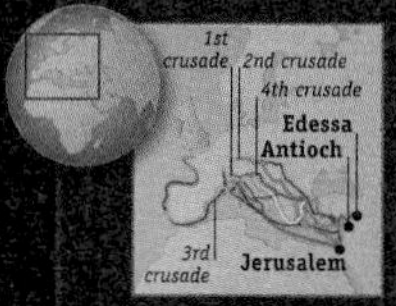

The Holy Land
The struggle to control the Holy Land lasted for 200 years.

Over the centuries, knights from different European countries fought one another for glory and riches. However, in 1095, many knights united when Pope Urban II declared the first of nine crusades to force Christianity on the Muslims of the Middle East. Jerusalem was a holy city for both religions, and it changed hands several times.

Crusader Richard I, king of England

SWORD-WIELDING KNIGHT

JOUSTING HELMET

ARMORED GAUNTLET

ARMOR
Full metal jacket
The knight's head and body were protected by metal plates, which were curved to deflect blows. The weak points were at the joints.

Headpiece
It was hot and hard to breathe inside the helmet, and the knight could see only straight ahead through the narrow slit. However, the full head protection meant that he could take his time in considering how best to attack.

21

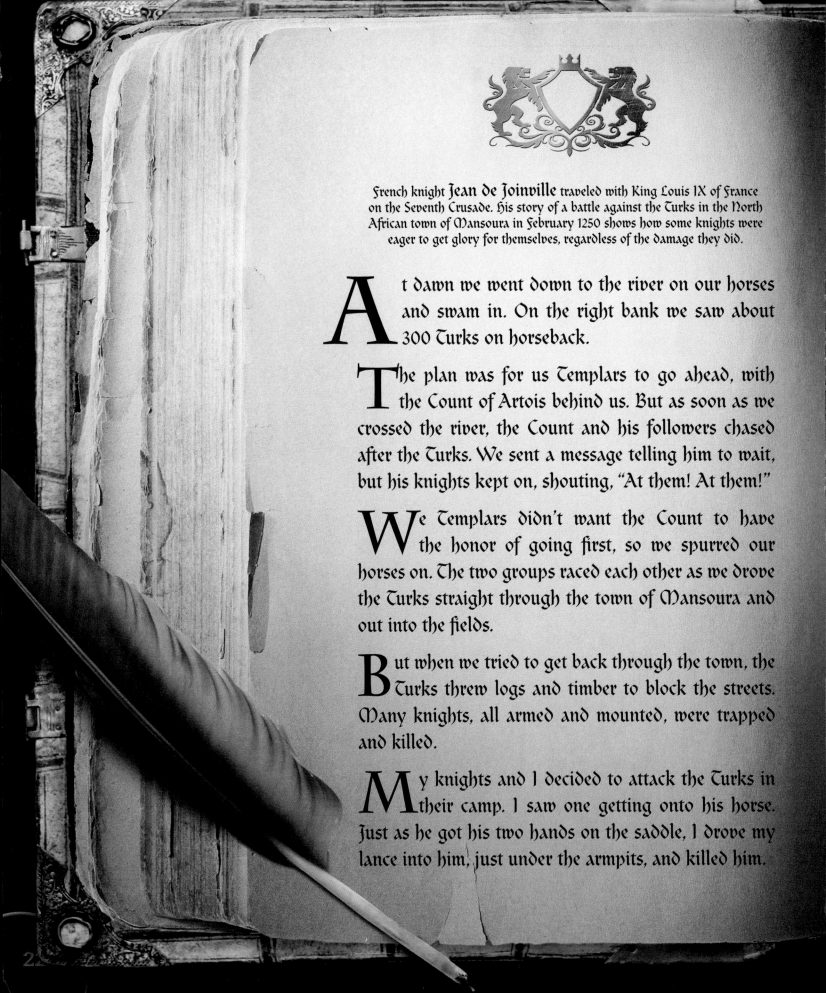

French knight **Jean de Joinville** traveled with King Louis IX of France on the Seventh Crusade. His story of a battle against the Turks in the North African town of Mansoura in February 1250 shows how some knights were eager to get glory for themselves, regardless of the damage they did.

At dawn we went down to the river on our horses and swam in. On the right bank we saw about 300 Turks on horseback.

The plan was for us Templars to go ahead, with the Count of Artois behind us. But as soon as we crossed the river, the Count and his followers chased after the Turks. We sent a message telling him to wait, but his knights kept on, shouting, "At them! At them!"

We Templars didn't want the Count to have the honor of going first, so we spurred our horses on. The two groups raced each other as we drove the Turks straight through the town of Mansoura and out into the fields.

But when we tried to get back through the town, the Turks threw logs and timber to block the streets. Many knights, all armed and mounted, were trapped and killed.

My knights and I decided to attack the Turks in their camp. I saw one getting onto his horse. Just as he got his two hands on the saddle, I drove my lance into him, just under the armpits, and killed him.

We charged through the camp, but in the fields outside we found 6,000 Turks, and they came charging at us. Lord Ralph was pulled off his horse, and we raced back to rescue him. The Turks threw spears and my horse fell to his knees, sending me flying over his ears. I picked myself up, with my shield hanging from my neck and my sword in my hand.

My knights came to help, and we ran into a ruined house. The Turks attacked on all sides, climbing the walls and thrusting down their spears. Lord Hugh got three wounds on his face. Lord Frederick got a gash between his shoulder blades so wide the blood flowed out as if a tap was running. Lord Erard received a sword cut across his face. Even so, he was able to ride off to get help.

Then the King and his whole battalion rode up with a great roar of trumpets and drums. He towered above his followers, with a gilded helmet on his head and a German sword in his hand. His champion knights fell upon the Turks, and the fight raged on with clubs and swords.

One of my squires brought me a pony, and I placed myself next to the King. In the battle, many of our people made a fine show. But others ran away from the fight and fled in panic. I could tell you some of their names, but I won't, because they are dead.

battle

CRÉCY, France, August 26, 1346

Edward III of England claimed the title of king of France because his mother, Isabella, was French. He sailed across the English Channel with an army of 16,000 soldiers and fought his way across northern France. French king Philip VI raised an army, and in 1346 the two forces clashed at Crécy.

King Edward III of England

King Philip VI of France

WHO WAS THERE?

	FRANCE		ENGLAND
FORCES	35,000	FORCES	16,000
CASUALTIES Killed	14,000	CASUALTIES Killed	200

2 The crossbowmen could not see properly because they were dazzled by sunlight. They rushed up the hill but turned back to escape the deadly English arrows. At the same time, the eager French knights decided to charge. They rode straight into their own crossbowmen.

Army formations
The French forces were made up of mounted knights, men-at-arms, and crossbowmen from Italy. The English had longbowmen, knights, and foot soldiers.

English overview
King Edward had a great view of the area from a windmill on the ridge.

On the ridge
The English placed their carts in a circle to protect equipment and horses.

Firepower
Edward's 10,000 longbowmen were able to fire every five seconds.

Longbow advantage
A longbow could be fired three times faster than a crossbow and had a range of 980 feet (300 m).

French leader
King Philip directed the rear guard from raised ground looking across the shallow valley.

Wadicourt

Estrees

Fontaine sur Maye

Mounted knights
The French cavalry followed the crossbowmen into battle, together with the men-at-arms.

Crécy

1 The English set up on a ridge near Crécy. They dug ditches and laid sets of spikes to slow any attack by the French. When he arrived, King Philip wanted to rest his tired army and fight the next day. But the French nobles wanted the glory of a quick victory, so their crossbowmen advanced on the English and fired.

French advance
The French lined up in rows, with crossbowmen in front. They launched a crossbow attack at 4:00 PM.

Bow mistake
The crossbowmen did not protect their weapons from the rain, so the bows were slack and the bolts fell short.

Close combat
English foot soldiers smashed hammers into the armor of the French knights, or stuck daggers between the joints.

Difficult terrain
The ground had been softened by rain, slowing the cavalry's horses.

Casualties
Arrows wounded the horses, which then fell, leaving French knights stranded on the ground.

Blocked route
Dead and injured crossbowmen and fallen knights blocked the way for the charging riders.

Over and over again
The French knights charged about 15 times, only stopping at midnight.

Cavalry charge
The knights charged with banners flying and swords raised. The English captured 80 of these banners.

3

The few French who managed to reach the English side had to deal with ditches and spikes in the ground. Then they met fresh and ruthless foot soldiers. When the battle ended during the night, about 14,000 of the French army lay dead.

Royal retreat
A wounded King Philip rode away around midnight, knowing that his army was totally defeated.

Final moments
The next morning, the English foot soldiers finished off the wounded still on the battlefield.

OUTCOME

The English army marched on the French port of Calais and began a siege, taking the town the next year. It became a base for years of attacks by the English on the rest of France. The successful use of the longbow by the English king ended the dominance of mounted knights in battles. For 50 years following the Battle of Crécy, knights dismounted from their horses to fight.

YARI, THE WARRIOR'S SPEAR

SAMURAI

Long spear
Samurai thrust their *yari* from horseback as well as fighting with them on the ground. It took great skill to kill with these long, heavy weapons.

Honor was more important than winning for the samurai of Japan. These warriors came from noble families and preferred to challenge people of equal rank in one-to-one combat. Sometimes the disgrace of losing was so great that the loser killed himself.

WAKIZASHI, FOR CLOSE COMBAT

Decoration
The square-shaped hilt and the scabbard of the *wakizashi* were often richly decorated, sometimes with the skin of a ray.

WAKIZASHI LACQUERED WOOD SCABBARD

KATANA, FOR OPEN COMBAT

Daisho (paired swords)
Swords were called "the soul of the samurai." They were fearsome, with razor-sharp stainless steel blades. A samurai would carry both a *katana* and a *wakizashi*.

KATANA LACQUERED WOOD SCABBARD

WEAPONS AND ARMOR
Quick on their toes
Samurai had lightweight armor so that they could move fast during sword fights. It was made of bamboo, cloth, and metal, and it was intended to impress as well as protect.

SAMURAI WITH *YUMI* (BOW)

United country
Tokugawa Ieyasu won a major battle in 1600 and ended the civil war to rule Japan.

Japan was a divided nation, where clans paid samurai to fight for them. Ninja sometimes fiercely defended their territories against the samurai. These local wars lasted for more than four centuries, until Japan was united under the first shogun, Tokugawa Ieyasu. After that, only samurai were allowed to carry arms.

Tokugawa Ieyasu, the first shogun

Antler crest
Horn and antler shapes helped identify the warrior.

Headpiece
Warriors cut off the heads of dead enemies, so samurai burned incense in their helmets. This made their heads smell nice.

Ninja

The Japanese name for these secret warriors is *shinobi*, which means "steal away." Their silent approach, extraordinary variety of killing weapons, and skill in martial arts made them formidable opponents.

HOOK SWORD

SHORT SWORD

SHURIKEN (THROWING STARS)

NINJA WITH *KATANA*

Face mask
Designed to look scary, the mask guarded the face and helped keep the helmet in place.

On horseback
Early samurai were experts at fighting from horseback. Their code of chivalry was called *kyuba no michi*— "the way of horse and bow."

Necklace
Leather encircling the neck was meant to keep the throat from being slit by a blade or arrow.

hand to hand

A modern soldier's view

In Japan, if a samurai failed in his mission, he may have had to commit suicide in order to maintain his honor. We don't have any equivalent ritual in our military. That said, honor is an important facet for any soldier in any conflict.

Today we conduct what is called an after-action review after a training mission or actual combat operation. The purpose of an AAR is so that the unit involved can review everything it did right and everything it did wrong. By doing an honest AAR after each mission, the unit is able to improve its performance.

—JACK MURPHY, FORMERLY OF THE 75TH RANGER REGIMENT AND SPECIAL FORCES

Seeking revenge
This battle scene is part of a story about 47 samurai, called ronin (masterless samurai) after their master was forced to kill himself in 1701. The faithful ronin sought revenge by attacking the castle of an official called Moronao.

Conquistador, Spain, 1519–1541

Weapon of choice
Crossbow bolts could be deadly at a distance of 900 feet (275 m). For close combat, the rapier was lethal against an opponent who wore no armor.

CROSSBOW

CONQUISTADOR

CONQUISTADOR FOOT SOLDIER

Conquistadors were battle-hardened, steel-encased warriors. They must have seemed invincible to the Aztecs and Incas of Central and South America. However, the deadly diseases that the Spanish carried killed more people than their swords ever did.

High crest
The comb ran from front to back. It strengthened and thickened the helmet where it was most vulnerable—at the center of the skull.

COMB MORION HELMET

STEEL SHIELD

PARTIZAN

WEAPONS AND ARMOR

Hitting hard and fast
The Spanish attacked fast on horseback and in full armor. They carried lethal weapons, including the partizan, which had a spearhead at its tip and a curved section underneath to parry blades.

RAPIER

Fine steel
A sword did not pass inspection until it could bend in a half circle and survive impact with a helmet.

CROSSBOW BOLTS

Conquerors
After Hernán Cortés brought about the fall of the Aztecs, the Spanish conquered most of South America.

Spanish conquistadors sailed across the Atlantic to conquer ancient civilizations such as the Maya and Aztecs of Central America and the Incas of South America. Although the Spanish claimed to want to convert people to Christianity, they did not settle the invaded lands. Instead, they enslaved the population and shipped huge amounts of gold and silver back home. In 100 years of Spanish rule, the population of South America fell from 50 million to 8 million, partly because the Spanish carried diseases that killed the native inhabitants.

Francisco Pizarro, Inca conqueror

Inca

The Incas had a highly trained army and were used to war. But their weapons were spears and axes made of wood and stone. They could not compete with the conquistadors' steel weapons.

STONE-HEADED CLUB

Metal skirt
Overlapping plates flexed to give complete protection to the warrior, whether on horseback or standing.

INCA PRIEST

Steel shell
Conquistadors wore heavy steel armor that was among the finest in the world. The Aztecs and Incas were unable to harm them.

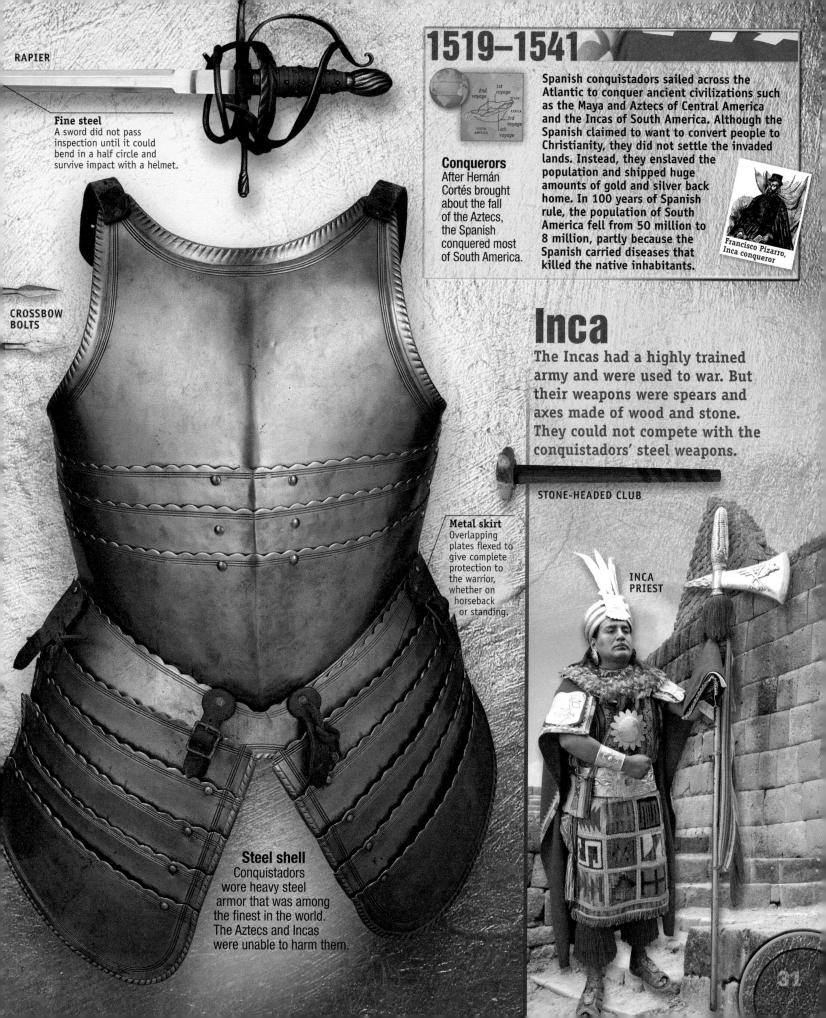

Next morning, September 5, 1519, we mustered the horses and every one of the wounded joined the ranks.

The crossbowmen were warned to use their supply of arrows very carefully, some of them loading while the others were shooting.

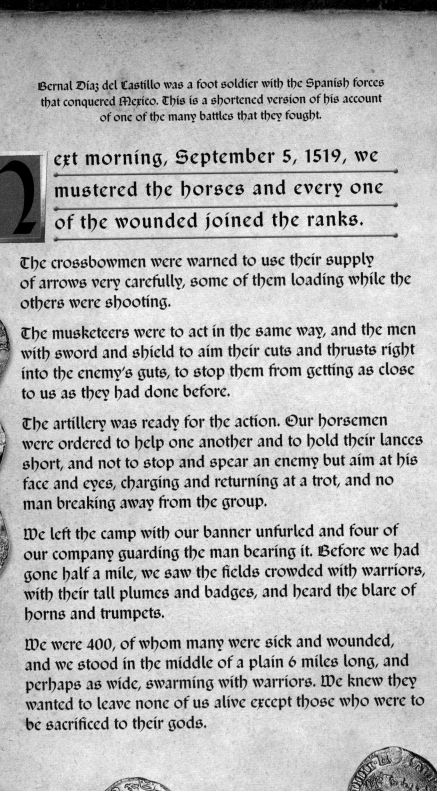

The musketeers were to act in the same way, and the men with sword and shield to aim their cuts and thrusts right into the enemy's guts, to stop them from getting as close to us as they had done before.

The artillery was ready for the action. Our horsemen were ordered to help one another and to hold their lances short, and not to stop and spear an enemy but aim at his face and eyes, charging and returning at a trot, and no man breaking away from the group.

We left the camp with our banner unfurled and four of our company guarding the man bearing it. Before we had gone half a mile, we saw the fields crowded with warriors, with their tall plumes and badges, and heard the blare of horns and trumpets.

We were 400, of whom many were sick and wounded, and we stood in the middle of a plain 6 miles long, and perhaps as wide, swarming with warriors. We knew they wanted to leave none of us alive except those who were to be sacrificed to their gods.

When they charged, the stones sped like hail from their slings, and their barbed and fire-hardened darts fell like corn on the threshing floor, each one capable of piercing any armor.

Their swordsmen and spearmen ran at us bravely, shouting and yelling. But steady work from our artillery, musketeers, and bowmen caused a lot of damage, and stout thrusts from our swords stopped their charging swordsmen. But they came at us in such numbers that only by a miracle of swordplay were we able to drive them back and re-form our ranks. One thing in our favor was that they were so crowded together that every shot hit more than one man.

They were afraid of our horses and our brave fighting with musket, sword, and crossbow. They tried to hide their losses, and whenever one of their men was wounded, they carried him off on their backs. The enemy lost heart, and when they realized that reinforcements were not coming to help, they retreated. Our horsemen followed them only a short distance, for they were too tired to ride far.

One of our men was killed, and 60 were wounded. All our horses were wounded, too. I was hit twice, once on the head by a stone, and once on the thigh by an arrow. But this did not stop me from fighting.

Landsknecht broadsword, 1600s
This massive German sword was wielded with two hands. Its straight, flat blade was perfect for snapping the ends off pikes and attacking charging horsemen.

Spanish partizan, ca. 1700
Foot soldiers used partizans—sharp metal blades mounted on long wooden poles. This weapon was up to 7 feet (2 m) long, with a double axhead under the blade.

Cup-hilt rapier, 1600s
This elegant weapon was also known as the Spanish rapier. It was perfect for fast, accurate thrusts, and the cup hilt protected the hand.

∨ M3 knife, 1940s
This was first issued to the US military in 1943, to be used by any soldier who did not have a bayonet.

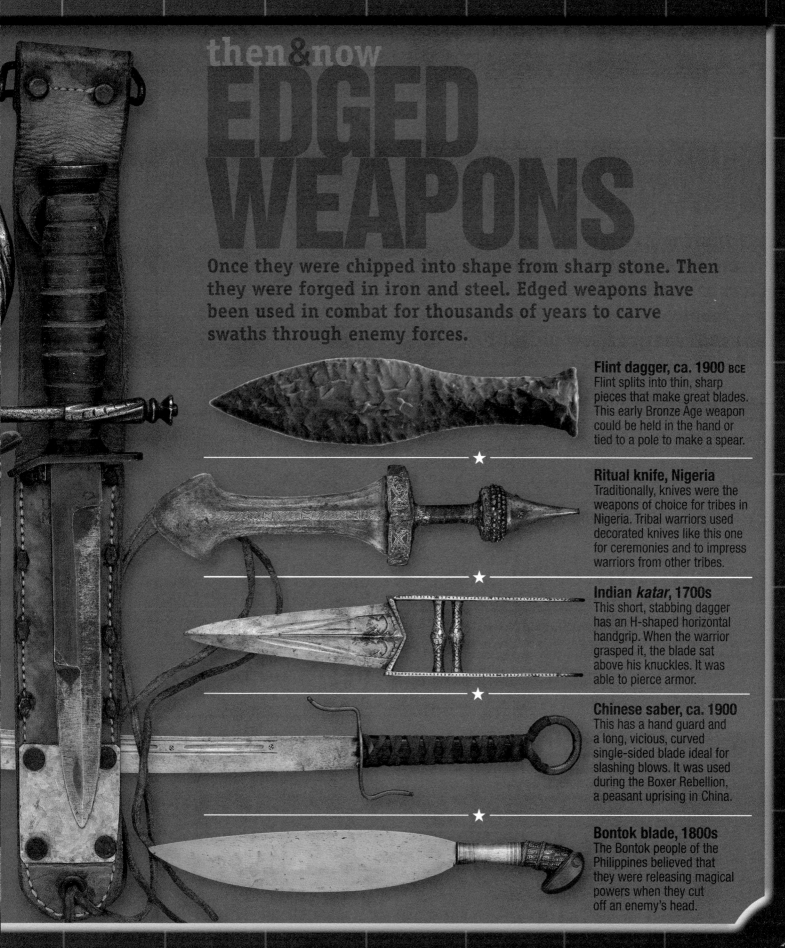

then&now
EDGED WEAPONS

Once they were chipped into shape from sharp stone. Then they were forged in iron and steel. Edged weapons have been used in combat for thousands of years to carve swaths through enemy forces.

Flint dagger, ca. 1900 BCE
Flint splits into thin, sharp pieces that make great blades. This early Bronze Age weapon could be held in the hand or tied to a pole to make a spear.

Ritual knife, Nigeria
Traditionally, knives were the weapons of choice for tribes in Nigeria. Tribal warriors used decorated knives like this one for ceremonies and to impress warriors from other tribes.

Indian *katar*, 1700s
This short, stabbing dagger has an H-shaped horizontal handgrip. When the warrior grasped it, the blade sat above his knuckles. It was able to pierce armor.

Chinese saber, ca. 1900
This has a hand guard and a long, vicious, curved single-sided blade ideal for slashing blows. It was used during the Boxer Rebellion, a peasant uprising in China.

Bontok blade, 1800s
The Bontok people of the Philippines believed that they were releasing magical powers when they cut off an enemy's head.

Priming pan
This contained a small amount of power that, when lit, ignited the powder in the barrel to fire out a lead ball.

Early musket.
In this gun, a burning piece of cord was lowered into a hole to light the powder in the priming pan.

Slow burner
The cord was held on a lever called a serpent.

FRENCH MUSKETEER

Flat stock
This was used as a club in hand-to-hand fighting.

Wheel lock
A spinning wheel caused a spark to fire the musket.

French musketeers were the special-ops troops of the 17th century. These highly trained royal bodyguards came mainly from rich families and were named after their new weapon, the musket. But they preferred the flash and dash of the rapier.

WEAPONS AND EQUIPMENT

Two-handed fighting
Although the musketeers were named for the musket, they mostly fought with a rapier in one hand and a dagger in the other.

Parrying dagger
A twist of the musketeer's wrist as an attacker's sword struck this dagger would unbalance the enemy. This gave the musketeer time to strike with the rapier.

Quillon
This crossbar extended from the hilt and blocked blows from an enemy. Wrapping his fingers around the quillon gave the musketeer better control.

MAIN GAUCHE (LEFT HAND) DAGGER

MATCHLOCK MUSKET

FEATHERED HAT

WHEEL-LOCK MUSKET

Ramrod
This pole was lifted out to push the gunpowder and lead ball down the barrel.

1622–1815

War zone
The Thirty Years' War (1618–1648) was a series of wars across central Europe.

The French musketeers were formed in 1622 as bodyguards for King Louis XIII. France was unsettled in the 17th century, and kings were in great danger from enemies from inside France as well as from other countries across Europe. Musketeers also served their kings in various battles, including in the Thirty Years' War.

King Louis XIII of France

Pommel
The metal cap balanced the weight of the blade, making it easier to aim.

Hilt
The cup-shaped hilt of the rapier gave extra protection for the hand.

How to fire a musket
Gunpowder was poured in, and a ramrod was used to push a lead bullet down the barrel. A rest held the heavy gun steady for firing.

Rapier
This long, thin, sharply pointed sword was flexible and used for thrusting blows. It was often used in duels.

Fact or fiction
Probably the most famous musketeers in the world are fictional. *The Three Musketeers*, a book by French author Alexandre Dumas, has been the basis for many films.

EVOLUTION
The firearm began as a simple tube, closed at one end. Inside, powder was lit to make a small explosion that fired a missile. Over the centuries, the technology improved to make the firing mechanism more reliable.

Matchlock
"Lock" refers to the mechanism that ignited the gunpowder. The "match" was the slow-burning cord.

Wheel lock
This used a fast-spinning wheel to create a spark to light the gunpowder.

Flintlock
This had a powerful spring to strike a flint and make a spark to light the powder.

Rifleman, America, 1775–1781

Hunting rifle
American woodsmen used hunting rifles to fire on British officers from far away. The rifles were far more accurate than muskets.

40-inch (1 m) barrel
The long barrel added power as more gunpowder burned to push the bullet out.

Butt trap
Inside the hollow butt were scraps of greased linen. These were wrapped around bullets for a tight fit in the barrel.

KNIFE IN SCABBARD

AMERICAN REVOLUTIONARY INFANTRYMAN

REVOLUTIONARY WAR RIFLEMAN

In 1775, rebel colonists began a battle for independence against Britain's colonial government on the east coast of America. The rebel riflemen matched the British army in both determination and tactics.

DRUM

Both sides
The infantries blasted at each other with muskets as fast as they could reload—up to four times a minute. Both sides were armed with "Brown Bess" muskets.

MUSKET BALL

AX

WEAPONS AND EQUIPMENT

Battle tactics
The Americans grew skilled at defending against frontal attacks. They ambushed, then escaped before a big battle could develop.

SWIVEL GUN

Rifling
Grooves inside the barrel spun the bullet, making it fly farther in a straight line.

KIT BAG

By the sea
The 13 colonies were on the east coast of America.

CANADA
Fort Ticonderoga
Saratoga • Lexington
Trenton • Brooklyn
• Yorktown
• Charleston

In 1775, 13 North American colonies rose up against British rule. In 1776, they declared their independence as the United States of America, gaining support from France two years later. After six years of war, in 1781, the outnumbered and trapped British finally surrendered to the Americans.

American general George Washington

British redcoats

These soldiers were well trained to make steady attacks from the front. They found it difficult to adapt to deal with the sniping and ambushing tactics of the Americans.

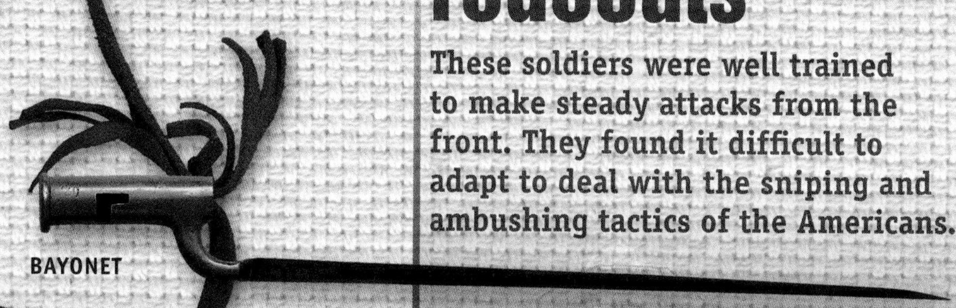

BAYONET

"BROWN BESS" MUSKET

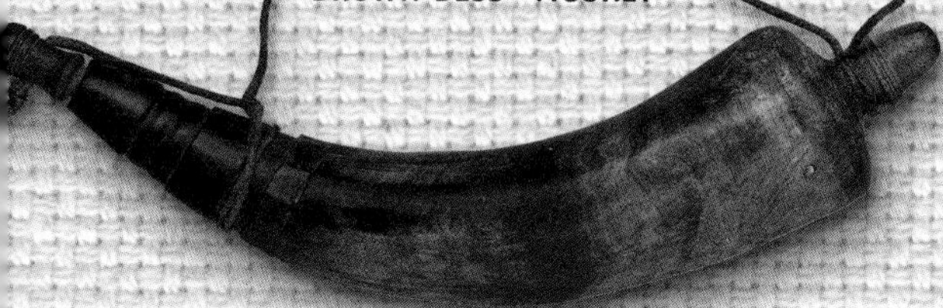

POWDER HORN

Surprise!
The colonists had learned how to make surprise attacks from their battles with Native Americans.

BRITISH INFANTRYMAN (REDCOAT)

GUN ON GARRISON CARRIAGE

FIELD GUN

39

under fire
A modern soldier's view

American riflemen required the qualities we most revere in American culture today: rugged individualism, creativity, bravery, and determination. The tactics used by the American patriots have much in common with modern military tactics that we would call maneuver warfare.

Having personally carried out ambushes, I can tell you that you first think about the technical aspects of the ambush. You think about setting in your machine gun where the gunner will have a strong sector of fire on the enemy as it comes down the road. You think about setting in your riflemen down behind the cover offered by trees, where they will be able to engage the enemy. Once your ambush is set in and you begin to wait, the human part of your brain kicks in. You're scared, because you know that you are about to be in a close-range firefight and that you will probably be killed. Then the third phase of thinking kicks in, and you just accept reality. You're a soldier, you have a job to do, and if you die doing it, then so be it.

—JACK MURPHY, FORMERLY OF THE 75TH RANGER REGIMENT AND SPECIAL FORCES

Lying in wait
A rifleman hid behind trees and walls until he got the chance to take a shot at an enemy, especially if the redcoat was an officer. The minute he fired his musket, the sparks and smoke gave away his hiding place.

battle

BUNKER HILL, Massachusetts, June 17, 1775

The American Revolution began when 13 colonies rose up to fight British rule. The British were soon trapped in Boston, where their supplies arrived by ship. If the colonists could fire down from a hill overlooking this key location, they could force the British out.

WHO WAS THERE?

![] AMERICAN COLONIES	![] GREAT BRITAIN
FORCES 1,400	FORCES 2,500
CASUALTIES	CASUALTIES
Killed 115	Killed 226
Wounded 305	Wounded 828

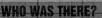
Fort Ticonderoga
Saratoga • Lexington
Trenton • Brooklyn
• Yorktown
• Charleston

William Howe, British major general

John Stark, American colonel

2 The British used 28 barges to land troops, who then marched uphill toward the Americans' position. The defenders waited until the redcoats were only 130 feet (40 m) away before blasting at them with their muskets. The troops who did not fall retreated and tried again. The same sequence of events was repeated, with more casualties.

Hand to hand
The Americans were short on training and equipment. The British redcoats, on the other hand, were used to close combat using bayonets.

1 **On the night** of June 16, American forces occupied hills looking over Boston Harbor. From there they would be able to fire cannons into Boston and at ships in the harbor. As soon as the British saw this, they knew that they must attack.

Bunker Hill
The American forces had been sent to build up abandoned British earthworks on Bunker Hill, but they decided that Breed's Hill was better, since it was closer to the harbor.

Rail fence
A stone-and-rail fence stretched from Breed's Hill down to the Mystic River.

Breed's Hill defense
A 136-foot-long (41.5 m) redoubt (earthwork fort) was built overnight.

Alert
At 4:00 AM on June 17, a British sailor on HMS *Lively* noticed troop movements on Breed's Hill and alerted his captain.

Protecting Boston
The city of Boston was occupied by 6,000 British troops, and British warships patrolled the waters that protected it.

Ships at risk
The Americans wanted to take Breed's Hill in order to fire artillery at the British ships that had control of Boston Harbor.

Mystic River
Bunker Hill
Breed's Hill
Charlestown
Boston

Targeting the enemy
The Americans could fire more accurately, because they could rest their rifles on the rail fence.

Side attack
Some British troops moved along the riverbank to try to catch the American left flank by surprise, but they were beaten back.

Retreat
The British made two attempts to take the hill but had to retreat each time with heavy losses.

Cannon fire
The British infantry came under fire, and the redcoats set the neighborhood of Charlestown on fire in an attempt to eliminate the enemy snipers.

Ships shell town
British ships also attacked the area with cannons.

Ships shell redoubt
While British troops were landing, their warships fired shells at the redoubt.

Redcoat advance
The British troops advanced up Breed's Hill. They marched in lines four men deep.

3 **The colonists** were running out of ammunition. When the British marched up the hill a third time, they reached the defenders. There was a brief hand-to-hand fight before the American forces surrendered their position.

Third time lucky
The British had the advantage of bayonets once they reached the redoubt, so they won the day.

Retreat
The Americans were able to get away, and the British did not chase after them.

Destruction
Charlestown and its wharves and dockyards had to be completely rebuilt.

OUTCOME

The British won—but at great cost. The Americans had shown that their inexperienced forces could take on the British army. The battle also helped the Americans realize that they needed to be better organized. For their part, the British now saw that the war was going to be long and tough. In March 1776, American guns placed on Dorchester Heights, south of Boston, forced the British to leave the city. They had lost a vital harbor and base.

Wire decoration
Tribes used different patterns on their weapons to identify themselves.

Iwisa or knobkerrie
The knob on the end of this heavy wooden rod turned it into a vicious club that a warrior swung to strike a powerful blow.

ZULU

ZULU CHIEF

Losing a battle to the Zulu of Africa meant certain death— they never took prisoners, and the bodies of enemies were cut open to release their spirits. Zulu warriors were famous for their "buffalo horn" formation: A large mass of warriors would advance, while groups on either side moved in to surround the enemy.

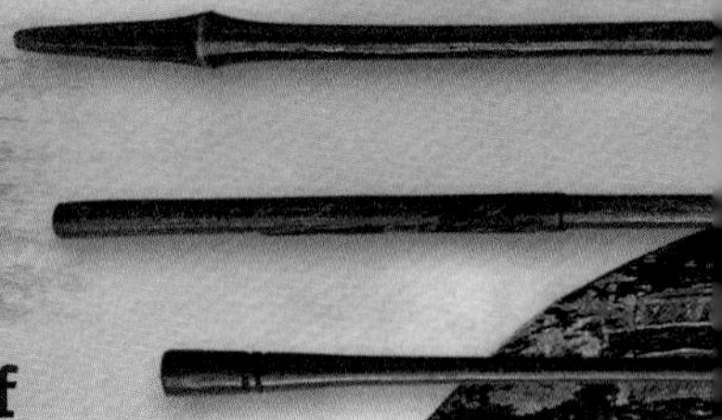

ISIHLANGU (OXHIDE SHIELD)

ISIZENZE (BATTLE-AX)

ISIZENZE (BATTLE-AX)

WEAPONS
Simple weaponry
The Zulu threw lightweight javelins or used shorter, large-bladed spears for stabbing. The shields were the property of the king and issued to troops when needed.

IPAPA OR ASSEGAIS (JAVELINS)

ISIHLANGU (OXHIDE SHIELD)

Territory
Zulu lands were at their greatest extent in the 1830s.

The Zulu began waging war on other tribes in 1816. Under the leadership of the powerful Shaka Zulu, they fought the Boers (Dutch settlers) in the 1830s and later the British army, which defeated them in 1879 and then took over their lands. With their spears and axes, the Zulu stood little chance against the enemy's deadly rifles.

Zulu king and conqueror Shaka

Boer

The Boers were African settlers originally from the Netherlands. They were very independent and refused to wear uniforms. They fired single-shot muskets at advancing Zulu warriors, mowing down huge numbers.

MARTINI-HENRY RIFLE

BOER SETTLER

Cured-hide shield
A Zulu warrior hit an opponent with the end point of his shield before going in with his spear. Younger warriors used darker shields.

A steel wheel spun against the mineral pyrite to make the spark that fired the pistol.

Some wheel lock pistols were richly decorated.

Flint held in hammer

Frizzen, or striking steel

German wheel lock, mid-1500s
This double-barreled pistol used a wheel to make a spark, instead of the slow-burning fuse of a matchlock pistol.

Trigger

Cavalryman's flintlock, ca. 1645
The flintlock got its name because it fired when a piece of hard flint rock struck a piece of steel. This made a spark that ignited gunpowder. This pistol was also called a dog lock because of the shape of the hammer.

Ammunition was stored, ready for loading, in a nonremovable box magazine.

German Mauser C96, 1900s
This self-loading pistol had a long barrel for greater accuracy. It was called the "broomhandle" because of its round wooden grip.

Tranter percussion revolver, late 1800s
Percussion revolvers had an advantage over guns with earlier firing mechanisms because they would fire in all weather conditions.

PISTOLS

In the mid-15th century, gunpowder was first put into the barrel of a handgun. This new, powerful weapon changed how wars were fought and evolved to become key equipment for modern armies.

A welded seam along the length of the barrel formed a strong tube.

Italian wheel lock, ca. 1660
Some of Leonardo da Vinci's drawings from around 1500 show early wheel lock designs, although these guns did not appear until 100 years later.

7-shot Mortimer flintlock, 1700s
Flintlocks took time to reload, so some special pistols that could fire multiple successive shots from a single barrel were made.

Turkish flintlock, late 1700s
The parts for this flintlock probably came from western Europe. Starting in the 1730s, Turkish warriors did not use the weapon often.

4-barreled pistol, ca. 1840
The soldier would first fire two barrels of this four-barreled "turnover" pistol. Then he rotated all four barrels in order to fire the other two.

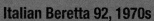

German Luger P08, 1900s
This was one of the first semiautomatic pistols that put the next cartridge in place as it fired. It was used by the German army in both world wars.

Italian Beretta 92, 1970s
This semiautomatic pistol was originally designed for the Italian army and police. In 1985, it became the standard sidearm of the US military.

MELEE SPEAR

Silent killer
Plains Indians often used a melee spear, also called a lance. It could be a silent missile, thrown with deadly accuracy, or be used as a thrusting weapon in close combat.

SIOUX

SIOUX CHIEF

Status symbol
Spears were decorated with buffalo fur, eagle feathers, and beads—or sometimes scalps taken from enemies.

Every day was a fighting day for the Sioux warrior, whether he was battling other tribes or taking on the invading white settlers to defend his family and lands. The buffalo-hunting skills of stealth and deadly accuracy with arrows and spears were just as effective when ambushing settlers and the US Army. The Sioux were skilled horsemen who attacked and got out fast, usually avoiding long battles.

WAR CLUB WITH STONE HEAD

Protection
The Sioux believed that their shields had great spiritual powers. Birds, animals, and other symbols were painted on a shield to protect its owner.

Scalping knife
A Sioux warrior used this knife to cut off the top of a dead enemy's head. The warriors kept scalps as trophies.

WEAPONS AND EQUIPMENT
Fighting power
Plains Indians had long-distance range with their spears and bows and arrows; they used lightweight tomahawks and axes for close combat. They also used rifles that they had captured from settlers or gotten in trades.

War and peace
Tomahawk means "war club" in the Powhatan language. This one is also a peace pipe.

PEACE PIPE TOMAHAWK

WOODEN SHIELD WITH EAGLE MOTIF

BOW

ARROWS IN QUIVER

1860s–1880s

Hunting buffalo
Before the settlers arrived, the Sioux traveled vast distances to hunt.

The Sioux tribes, like other Plains Indians, fought bravely for more than 20 years as their hunting lands were invaded by settlers and the US Army. But the Sioux were outgunned by the well-equipped troops, who destroyed the buffalo that the Sioux relied on for food.

Chief Red Cloud of the Sioux

US Cavalry

The US Cavalry was led by officers who had fought in the American Civil War (1861–1865). They adapted their tactics to fight the fast-moving Plains Indians, and they had the advantage of far better firepower.

COLT 1851 NAVY REVOLVER

CORPORAL CAVALRYMAN

Fast and deadly
Sioux bows were double curved, making them very powerful. Skilled marksmen could fire arrows every few seconds, with a range of 600 feet (180 m).

49

SPRINGFIELD RIFLE

Union rifle
The American-made Springfield rifle accurately fired a new type of bullet. A minié ball could break a man's bones even if he was 1,000 feet (300 m) away.

MINIÉ BALL

UNION (NORTHERN) INFANTRYMAN

CIVIL WAR INFANTRYMAN

In the American Civil War, lines of soldiers marched across open ground into a hail of bullets and shells. When close enough, they stabbed with bayonets fixed to their rifles. About 750,000 died, half from disease.

CONFEDERATE SWORD A

UNION CUP

BONE-HANDLED PENKNIFE

CONFEDERATE KIT BAG

CONFEDERATE WATER BOTTLE

CS

KEEPSAKE

UNION COLT DRAGOON REVOLVER

CONFEDERATE LEMAT REVOLVER

EVERYDAY LIFE
Heavy packs
Union troops marched with 50 pounds (23 kg) of gear, often dumping things to reduce the load. The Confederates had fewer supplies and did not wear standard uniforms.

WEAPONS
Firepower
The main weapon for both sides was the musket rifle, which could be fired three to four times a minute. Cannons were also effective.

1861–1865

SPRINGFIELD BAYONET

ENFIELD SHORT RIFLE

Confederate rifle
The British-made Enfield used the same ammunition that the Springfield did. Both rifles needed animal fat or beeswax to keep their barrels well greased.

UNION SWORD AND SCABBARD

CABBARD

CONFEDERATE BOWIE KNIFE

War zone
There were 23 Union states and 11 Confederate.

The American Civil War was fought because of a deep divide between the Northern and Southern states. The North wanted to abolish slavery and was united under a federal government led by President Abraham Lincoln. The South's economy was based on slave labor, and those states wanted to keep their ability to make their own decisions. In 1861, this erupted into civil war. On April 9, 1865, after four years of bloody battle, the Confederate (Southern) forces surrendered to the Union (Northern) army.

Union general Ulysses S. Grant

Confederate general Robert E. Lee

CONFEDERATE (SOUTHERN) INFANTRYMAN

Loading the barrels
A carousel magazine dropped new cartridges into each of the six barrels as they revolved.

12-pounder cannon
The Confederates made good use of this cannon. It was light enough to be pulled by a team of horses, but it had the power to destroy fortifications half a mile (0.8 km) away.

Spitting fire
Starting in 1864, some Union forces had extra firepower with the Gatling gun. It had ten barrels that were turned by a handle to fire 250 rounds a minute.

Ammunition
Cartridges for this forerunner to the machine gun were carried in a wooden box.

team spirit

A modern soldier's view

I think team spirit and personal courage are both required, whether you're fighting today, in the Civil War, or with Alexander against the Persians. You can't have one without the other. Without personal courage, you would never charge the enemy. Without team spirit, you would never attack, because you wouldn't trust the soldiers to your left and right.

Disease from infected wounds and bad hygiene killed more people than bullets did during the Civil War. The importance of proper medical care cannot be emphasized enough, especially in today's conflicts. First responder training teaches every one of our soldiers how to apply basic lifesaving techniques, like tying a tourniquet on an amputated limb. A lot of our troops who would have died if they'd received their injuries in the Vietnam War are now able to come home alive because our medical training has improved so much.

—JACK MURPHY, FORMERLY OF THE 75TH RANGER REGIMENT AND SPECIAL FORCES

The calm before the storm
These Union soldiers are resting in a trench at Fredericksburg, VA, in December 1862. They later launched several attacks that failed, and they suffered terrible casualties.

IN 1863, **TILLIE PIERCE** WAS ONLY 15 YEARS OLD
WHEN THE CIVIL WAR REACHED HER HOMETOWN OF
GETTYSBURG, IN THE UNION STATE OF PENNSYLVANIA.
WHAT FOLLOWED WAS ONE OF THE MOST IMPORTANT
AND DECISIVE BATTLES OF THE WAR. IT BROUGHT VICTORY
AND A CHANGE OF FORTUNE FOR THE UNION.

Soon the town was filled with infantry, and then the searching
and ransacking began. They wanted horses, clothing, anything and
almost everything they could conveniently carry away.

The Union troops built these
temporary entrenchments
near Gettysburg.

We frequently saw the Rebels [Confederates]
riding our horse up and down the street, until
at last she became so lame she could hardly get
along. That was the last we saw of her, and I felt
that I had been robbed of a dear friend.

[During the second day of the battle:]
Several field officers came into the house and
asked permission to go on the roof in order
to make observations. I was told to show
them the way up. They opened a trap door and
looked through their field glasses at the grand
panorama spread out below. The country for miles around seemed
to be filled with troops; artillery moving here and there as fast
as they could go; long lines of infantry forming into position;
officers on horseback galloping hither and thither! It was a
grand and awful spectacle.

[When the fighting was nearly over:]
We passed through a strip of woods where, some of the soldiers
told us, there had been a cavalry fight just an hour previous.

Here I first saw Rebel prisoners; there was a whole field filled with them. Their appearance was very rough, and they seemed completely tired out.

While we were talking with our soldiers, I noticed one eating a "hard tack." I, having nothing to eat as yet that day, and being quite hungry, must have looked very wistfully at him, for he reached into his haversack and presented me with one of those army delicacies. I accepted it with thanks, and nothing that I can recall was ever more relished, or tasted sweeter, than that Union soldier's biscuit eaten on July 3, 1863.

[When the troops were leaving:]

When Colonel Colvill and his attendants left our house, one of the men who had been nursing him presented me with a gun and bayonet, saying: "If any one comes after it, and wants to take it from you, just tell them that the gun was bought and paid for by the soldier who gave it to you."

It was not long before two soldiers called. I suppose I had been bragging too much about my relic. I said: "If they are mean enough to take the gun, they can have it; but it is *my* gun."

They seemed sorry as they rode away with my highly prized treasure. About two hours after this, I saw the same two soldiers returning on horseback, one of them having a gun on his shoulder. I went to the door and found these same men looking quite pleased as they said to me: "The Provost Marshal heard you were such a good Union girl, he has sent back your gun, and we are very happy to return it to you."

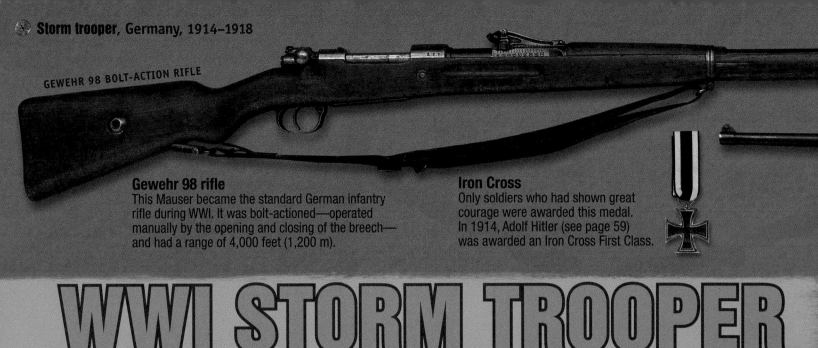

GEWEHR 98 BOLT-ACTION RIFLE

Gewehr 98 rifle
This Mauser became the standard German infantry rifle during WWI. It was bolt-actioned—operated manually by the opening and closing of the breech—and had a range of 4,000 feet (1,200 m).

Iron Cross
Only soldiers who had shown great courage were awarded this medal. In 1914, Adolf Hitler (see page 59) was awarded an Iron Cross First Class.

WWI STORM TROOPER

These German "shock troops," called *Stosstruppen*, changed the way in which wars were fought. In the trench warfare of World War I, whole armies camped in defensive positions. But the well-trained storm troopers smashed through the enemy's defenses and caused chaos. This powerful new tactic nearly won the war for the German army.

MAUSER KAR 98AZ CARBINE

New firepower
This first submachine gun fired bursts at 450 rounds a minute and was light enough to take into trench assaults.

Belt hook
Troops carried stick grenades on their belts or in small sacks.

WEAPONS AND EQUIPMENT

Battle tactics
Storm troopers prepared in darkness, and at dawn they launched speedy, fierce attacks with the newly developed weapons of grenades, flamethrowers, and light machine guns.

Key weapon
Each storm trooper carried up to 12 stick grenades. He lobbed these into enemy defenses before jumping in to finish off the dazed and deafened survivors.

This global war was fought mainly in Europe. It saw trench warfare, with rifles, machine guns, and artillery fired across the "no-man's-land" between the two sides. Storm troopers were used with great success starting in 1917, but the Germans began to lose when US troops joined the fight against them in the summer of 1918.

War zone
Storm troopers led a German push, but they could not keep front-line troops supplied.

Storm trooper leader General Oskar Emil von Hutier

Take aim
The wooden shoulder stock allowed the soldier to steady his aim.

Sharp tool
The detachable bayonet was used as a tool in camp as well as for fighting.

LUGER P08 WITH SHOULDER STOCK

Firepower
The "snail drum" magazine held 32 rounds.

BERGMANN MP18/I

"SNAIL DRUM" MAGAZINE

Hard hat
The helmet was shaped to protect the back of the neck.

Camouflage
Painted-on patterns like these were the first large-scale use of camouflage.

Armor
At first, storm troopers tried using steel shields, and later armor. However, these were heavy and slowed them down.

ENTRENCHING TOOL

British soldier

British soldiers were nicknamed Tommies, since *Tommy* was a common name at the time. They learned how to live in muddy trenches and to advance as shells were fired over their heads onto the enemy.

LEE-ENFIELD WITH BAYONET

WEBLEY MK VI

TRENCH CLUB

MK 1 GRENADE

Targeting
The front and back sights were fixed, preadjusted for a distance of 300 feet (90 m).

Foregrip
This removable wooden stock slid onto the barrel.

MAGAZINE

Sten gun
This submachine gun was lightweight and compact. A paratrooper fired it from the hip as he attacked.

WWII BRITISH PARATROOPER

BRITISH PARATROOPER

Paratroopers were a new kind of warrior in World War II. They dropped from the skies right into danger behind enemy lines. Their missions were to capture critical targets such as bridges so that troops on the ground could advance.

FAIRBAIRN–SYKES FIGHTING KNIFE

Cheek rest
This rifle's modifications, including the cheek rest, made it one of the best sniper rifles of WWII.

Welbike speed
This motorcycle, dropped by parachute, allowed troops to get moving quickly.

Folding bicycle
When parachuting, a paratrooper held this lightweight bike in his hands for a quick getaway.

TRANSPORT

Coming in to land
Troops were carried behind enemy lines in planes, then jumped from as low as 500 feet (150 m). Some floated silently in gliders to land in fields.

WEAPONS AND

Traveling light
They couldn't take heavy gear, since they needed to move fast. Compass to help them find the targets were k

Bayonet
The webbing allowed the spike bayonet to be pulled out quickly.

Suspenders
These held all the different elements of the webbing in place.

Webbing
Paratroopers traveled light, with everything they needed strapped to their bodies.

Waist belt
Two pouches were used for an emergency ration pack or equipment.

Water bottle
This held 2 pints (1 L) of water.

Entrenching tool
This consisted of a blade and a handle and was used to dig shelters and defenses.

LEE-ENFIELD SNIPER RIFLE

MILLS BOMB (GRENADE)

COMPASS

FIELD BINOCULARS

EQUIPMENT

1939–1945

World War II was one of the toughest wars that the world had ever experienced. It began in Europe, when Germany, led by Adolf Hitler, invaded Poland, but then it spread across the globe. In Europe, as the war raged between Germany and the Allies, British and US paratroopers played an important role. During the invasion of Normandy in June 1944, when the Allies began to take back German-occupied western Europe, the paratroopers' mission was to disrupt communications and ambush enemy troops.

German leader
Adolf Hitler

German infantry

Germany stormed across Europe quickly with blitzkrieg ("lightning war") tactics. German bombing raids followed by paratrooper drops cleared the way for tanks.

MAUSER K98 SNIPER RIFLE

WALTHER P38 PISTOL

BNZ MP40 SUBMACHINE GUN

WEHRMACHT INFANTRYMAN

battle

OMAHA BEACH, France, June 6, 1944

The only way to defeat the forces led by Adolf Hitler and end the fighting in Europe quickly was for the Allies to send a huge army to push the Germans back across the continent. The landing of Allied troops in France on D-Day was the biggest invasion using ships in the history of warfare.

WHO WAS THERE?

Allied forces

USA

UK

CANADA

FORCES 130,000

CASUALTIES
Killed or wounded 8,500

Axis forces

GERMANY

FORCES 50,000

CASUALTIES
Killed or wounded
Up to 9,000

Anti-landing defenses
The Germans laid obstructions and traps in the shallow water near the beaches to slow any landing craft.

Unsuccessful bombing
Bombers dropped 13,000 bombs that destroyed roads, railways, and bridges. But bad weather kept them from hitting the German defenses.

Shelling from the sea
Warships out at sea blasted shells at the German defenses, but they were well dug in and not badly damaged.

German defenses
The Germans' positions above the beach were linked by trenches so that fresh troops could replace casualties.

1

All the ports were well defended, so the Allied plan was to land troops on a stretch of five beaches along 50 miles (80 km) of the French coast in Normandy. The code names for these five beaches were Omaha and Utah (US troops), Juno (Canadian troops), and Gold and Sword (British troops).

US seaborne forces
Ships carried 23,250 for Utah and 43,250 for Omaha. The soldiers moved to landing craft 11 miles (18 km) out.

British and Canadian forces
These forces totaled 24,790 men for Gold, 21,400 for Juno, and 28,845 for Sword.

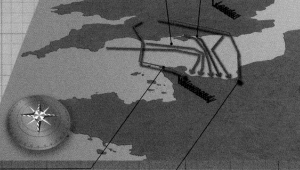

US airborne forces
15,000 US paratroopers, carrying their own weight in equipment, were dropped behind German lines.

British airborne forces
7,900 British paratroopers landed to protect the western end of the invasion area.

2

During the first landings, Omaha Beach saw the toughest fighting of all. There were more German defenders than expected, firing across the beach from 150-foot (45 m) cliffs. Many of the young US soldiers had never seen combat but were up against battle-hardened German troops.

Amphibious landing
At 6:30 AM, the first US troops jumped into the water from landing craft.

Watery graves
Weighed down by their gear and pulled along by the current, some soldiers drowned.

No cover
Between the shore and a bank of pebbles was open space, with nowhere to hide from the German machine guns.

3

The second wave of landings began at 7:00 AM. Again, troops faced a blizzard of enemy fire, and US forces were pinned down for seven hours. But by nightfall, 34,000 men had made it ashore.

Out of position
The strong current pulled the landing craft along the coast, so many landed much farther east than planned.

Pinned down
Soldiers who made it onto the beach sheltered behind a sea wall. Groups of rangers crept up the edge of the bay to attack the German positions.

Last stand
By the end of the day, about a fifth of the German soldiers were dead and reinforcements could not reach the area.

Deadly traffic jam
US vehicles trying to make it up the beach got trapped behind those in front that had been hit.

Progress inland
At 11:30 AM, shells from the US destroyer *McCook* took out a key gun emplacement, so troops and vehicles had a route off the beach.

Bridgeheads
More gaps were blasted through the German defenses, allowing US troops to attack their strongholds from behind.

Advance
A US message sent at 1:09 PM reported: "Troops formerly pinned down on beaches . . . advancing."

4

After five days of fighting, the five invasion sites were linked into one large beachhead where the waiting army could land. The Allies were now ready to take back Europe.

Mulberry harbor
One of two artificial harbors was sited at Omaha Beach so that more troops and supplies could be landed.

Beaches taken
Over the following days, the Allied forces combined and began to fan out from the five beaches.

Protection
By June 15, the Allies had control of the whole peninsula. This gave them a defensive line to protect the beaches from counterattacks.

Heading for Berlin
The Allied forces split up to take different routes across Europe. The war was not over, and there were still many battles to fight.

OUTCOME

D-Day did not end the war, but it was the beginning of the end for Adolf Hitler. By the end of June, 850,000 men and 150,000 Allied vehicles were on mainland Europe, and 2 million troops were eventually part of the Allied army that fought its way across Europe, freeing Paris in August and reaching the German border in September. With Russia advancing from the east, Hitler was trapped in Berlin. Germany surrendered in May 1945.

Game changer
The M16 was developed for the US Air Force and then issued to all troops sent to Vietnam. It used aircraft-grade aluminum and plastic, making it lighter than other weapons.

Flash hider

M16 RIFLE

Direct hit
The marine could accurately target someone at up to 1,800 feet (550 m).

Carrying handle

Magazine
Fed by the magazine, the rifle could fire up to 60 rounds a minute.

US MARINE, VIETNAM

US MARINE

The Marine Corps is the first US armed force to be sent into action abroad. For 20 years during the Vietnam War, nearly 500,000 marines supplied ground and air support to the South Vietnamese in their fight with the Communist Viet Cong.

Slot for plant camouflage

M1 HELMET

FLAK JACKET

WATER BOTTLE

M60 LIGHT MACHINE GUN

MACHETE

KA-BAR KNIFE AND SHEATH

EVERYDAY LIFE

Daily dangers
Marines had to deal with bugs, snakes, heat, and diseases such as malaria, as well as enemy mines and booby traps.

EQUIPMENT

Jungle warfare
Each marine carried 80 pounds (36 kg) of gear—a tough task in jungle conditions. Keeping weapons clean and dry was difficult.

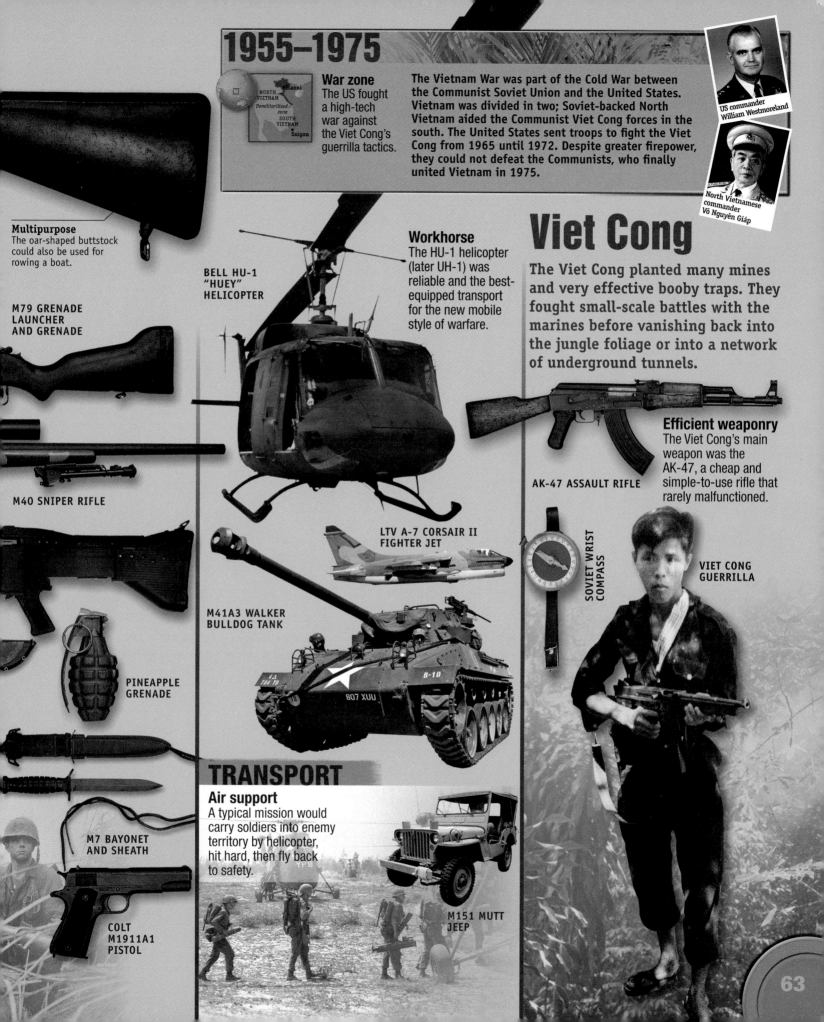

1955–1975

War zone
The US fought a high-tech war against the Viet Cong's guerrilla tactics.

The Vietnam War was part of the Cold War between the Communist Soviet Union and the United States. Vietnam was divided in two; Soviet-backed North Vietnam aided the Communist Viet Cong forces in the south. The United States sent troops to fight the Viet Cong from 1965 until 1972. Despite greater firepower, they could not defeat the Communists, who finally united Vietnam in 1975.

US commander William Westmoreland

North Vietnamese commander Võ Nguyên Giáp

Multipurpose
The oar-shaped buttstock could also be used for rowing a boat.

M79 GRENADE LAUNCHER AND GRENADE

M40 SNIPER RIFLE

BELL HU-1 "HUEY" HELICOPTER

Workhorse
The HU-1 helicopter (later UH-1) was reliable and the best-equipped transport for the new mobile style of warfare.

Viet Cong

The Viet Cong planted many mines and very effective booby traps. They fought small-scale battles with the marines before vanishing back into the jungle foliage or into a network of underground tunnels.

AK-47 ASSAULT RIFLE

Efficient weaponry
The Viet Cong's main weapon was the AK-47, a cheap and simple-to-use rifle that rarely malfunctioned.

LTV A-7 CORSAIR II FIGHTER JET

SOVIET WRIST COMPASS

VIET CONG GUERRILLA

M41A3 WALKER BULLDOG TANK

PINEAPPLE GRENADE

M7 BAYONET AND SHEATH

TRANSPORT

Air support
A typical mission would carry soldiers into enemy territory by helicopter, hit hard, then fly back to safety.

COLT M1911A1 PISTOL

M151 MUTT JEEP

63

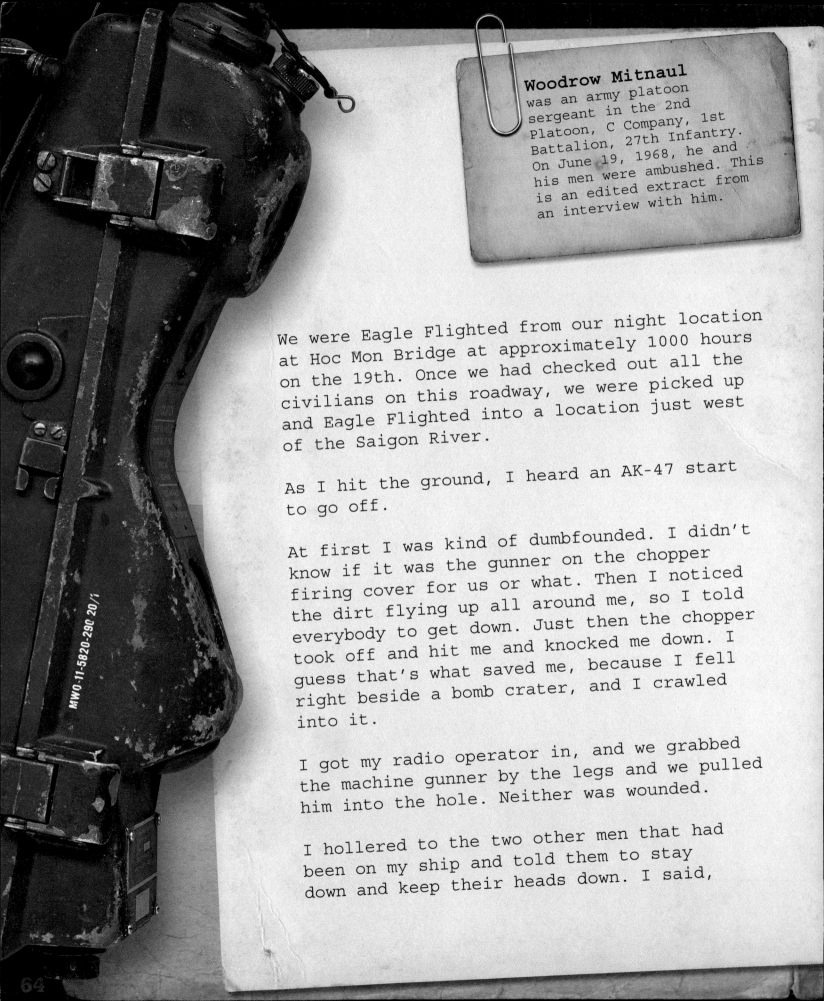

We were Eagle Flighted from our night location
at Hoc Mon Bridge at approximately 1000 hours
on the 19th. Once we had checked out all the
civilians on this roadway, we were picked up
and Eagle Flighted into a location just west
of the Saigon River.

As I hit the ground, I heard an AK-47 start
to go off.

At first I was kind of dumbfounded. I didn't
know if it was the gunner on the chopper
firing cover for us or what. Then I noticed
the dirt flying up all around me, so I told
everybody to get down. Just then the chopper
took off and hit me and knocked me down. I
guess that's what saved me, because I fell
right beside a bomb crater, and I crawled
into it.

I got my radio operator in, and we grabbed
the machine gunner by the legs and we pulled
him into the hole. Neither was wounded.

I hollered to the two other men that had
been on my ship and told them to stay
down and keep their heads down. I said,

"Stay low and wait until they bring smoke in, and then we can pull back to where we can do something."

We crossed lakes and streams as we followed the trail left by the Viet Cong.

Every time I'd move my head, machine-gun fire would open up. You could almost feel the powder. That's how close they were on us. Any time a man moved, they'd zap him.

I noticed that they were throwing out hand grenades from the bunker to my left. I said to my radio operator, "I pray to God they don't throw any out this way, because if they do we're gone." Because that's how close we were on them. There wasn't a thing we could do.

I guess about 20 minutes had elapsed, and finally I saw an Eagle Flight coming in, and the gunships came in and dropped smoke. Then they got artillery in there, and more gunships. Everything was dropping in on Charlie [the Viet Cong].

After they'd made these strikes, that's when Delta Company started sweeping from the right flank, but they didn't get too far in. They ran into fire from across the blue on the opposite side, sniper fire, and they ran into AK-47s that were in these bunkers up ahead. That's when they had to stop and pull back.

65

HELMETS

Helmets were designed specifically to save a soldier's most important asset—his head! And they changed as war changed, first protecting against swords and later against bullets.

Roman gladiator, ca. 100 CE
This bronze helmet was designed to deflect blows to the top of the skull. It also protected the neck and shoulders.

Anglo-Saxon, early 600s
Decorated with images of heroic warriors, this helmet was buried with the body of a king.

Spanish comb morion, 1500s
The comb, or crest, makes this helmet stronger. This style was popular all across Europe.

Closed helmet, 1600s
This helmet's visor is lockable. The slots let air in so the knight could breathe.

Samurai headpiece, 1700s
This elaborate helmet was not just for protection—the horns also show status. The face is made of metal. The neck guard is leather.

Iranian, 1600s
This is a "turban helmet" because the twists imitate the folds of a turban. These helmets were worn by the cavalry.

Prussian, 1800s
This helmet is polished steel, but many others were made of boiled leather and had a metal trim.

Soviet, 1940s
Steel was the best material for stopping the small metal pieces of shrapnel in World War II.

<< German, 1500s
Some closed helmets were decorated with strange faces. These would intimidate any enemy.

< US Air Force pilot's helmet, present
Besides protecting the pilot from impact, this lightweight helmet blocks noise and bright light. An oxygen mask can be added to it.

HK MP5K-N SUBMACHINE GUN

Shooting
The HK MP5K-N (left) was specially developed for Navy SEALs. It is very accurate because it hardly moves when fired, unlike many other guns. The HK MP5SD (right) is the silenced version of the HK MP5 series.

Silent weapon
The integrated silencer suppresses muzzle flash, so the weapon is great for night operations.

NAVY SEAL

Navy SEALs are the toughest warriors in the world, carrying out missions at sea, in the air, and on land. These highly skilled special-operations soldiers are trained to be ready for anything, from rescuing hostages to spying on enemy convoys.

FLASH GRENADE

GERBER

GERBER FOLDING KNIFE

MULTI-TOOL

BOLT CUTTERS

BLACKHAWK DYNAMIC ENTRY
NOTHING SHALL STAND IN YOUR WAY
BLACKHAWK.COM / 800-692-5925

EQUIPMENT
Well equipped
SEALs carry bolt cutters to get through fences, flash grenades to stun their targets, and combat knives for close fighting.

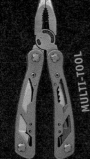

SOG COMBAT KNIFE

SEALs are often the first to arrive wherever US forces are sent. They have had some of the toughest military training in the world. Based at the Naval Amphibious Base in Coronado, CA, SEALs are trained to overcome obstacles that test their stamina, leadership, and ability to work as a team. Over the years, SEALs have carried out missions in many countries around the world, including Grenada, Afghanistan, Pakistan, Iran, Korea, Iraq, Kuwait, and Somalia.

Flexible firing
The gun fires either single bullets, bursts of 3, or 800 rounds a minute.

HK MP5SD
SUBMACHINE GUN

HK MK23 SOCOM PISTOL
WITH SILENCER

REMINGTON M700
BOLT-ACTION RIFLE

M249 MINIMI
MACHINE GUN

M16/M4 ASSAULT RIFLE

WEAPONS
Fighting force
SEALs can choose from a range of weapons, to use from far away or close-up and silently. Many have been designed specifically for the SEALs.

Amphibious force
SEALs are said to have "one foot in the water" because they often arrive by boat. The enemy rarely sees them coming before they actually attack.

secret force
A modern soldier's view

A Navy SEAL must have endurance, fortitude, a never-quit attitude, courage, a high level of athletic conditioning, and determination. It takes a lot of difficult training to become a SEAL, and a soldier must have motivation, preparation, and discipline to first complete the training and then carry out the work of a successful Navy SEAL.

Navy SEALs work in small units, which makes it easier to fight because you are fighting for your brother, with whom you have spent so much time and shared so many experiences. You know that you often have only each other, and so must fight even harder and with even more determination and ferocity.

—JEFF BUTLER, FORMER NAVY SEAL OFFICER

Hard training
A Navy SEAL emerges from the water during tactical warfare training. The soldiers need to train all the time so that they are in peak physical and mental condition and can operate with the greatest efficiency.

Sharp shooter
The gun is called the "light 50" because it is lightweight but uses high-impact .50-caliber ammunition.

Carrying handle

M107
SEMIAUTOMATIC
RIFLE

Folded support
These feet are spiked so that they grip the ground and hold the gun steady.

DESERT SOLDIER

Webbing pouches
These hold what the soldier needs for survival, including water, ammunition, first-aid supplies, and emergency rations.

The desert is a tough place to fight. Fierce heat and dust take their toll on soldiers and their equipment. It is vital that these warriors have reliable weaponry that is light enough to carry all day long but has the power to take out armored vehicles.

WEBBING WITH ATTACHED GRENADES

EQUIPMENT

Adapting to the climate
In the heat, it is important that soldiers wear clothing that "breathes," to avoid overheating, and have a constant supply of water.

ADVANCED COMBAT HELMET (ACH)
WITH NIGHT-VISION MONOCULAR

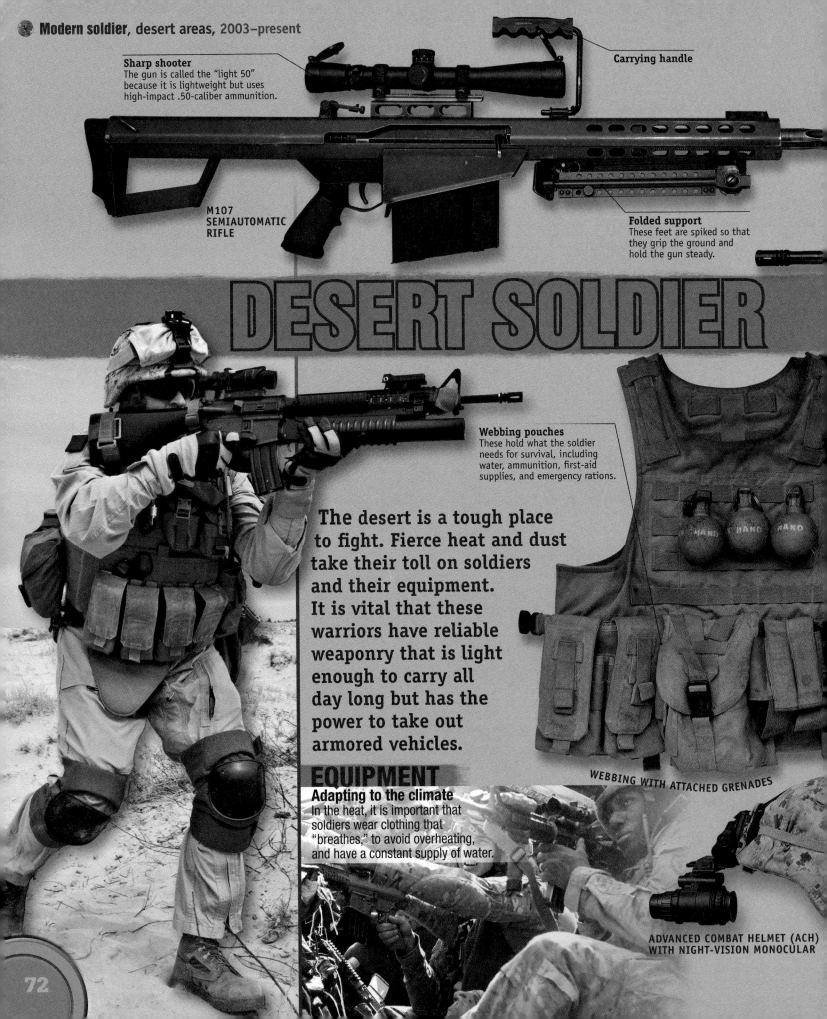

Long shot
The M107 has a range of 8,000 feet (2,430 m). It is so powerful that it can stop an armored car or hit a person through a wall.

Close-quarters combat
A CQC rifle is a favorite with special-ops soldiers. It can be fitted with barrels of different sizes.

M67 FRAGMENTATION GRENADE

2003–present
The 1990–1991 Gulf War was sparked by Iraq's invasion of Kuwait in August 1990, which forced the United Nations to intervene. The war between Iraq and forces sent by the United Nations saw more than 100,000 air strikes in Operation Desert Storm, plus a four-day ground offensive. In 2003, 12 years later, the US and British armies invaded Iraq, eventually bringing about the capture and death of Iraqi president Saddam Hussein.

Saddam Hussein, president of Iraq

BOEING AH-64 APACHE ATTACK HELICOPTER

F-15 EAGLE FIGHTER JET

LEG HOLSTER WITH BERETTA M9

BAYONET AND HOLSTER

HIGH-MOBILITY MULTIPURPOSE WHEELED VEHICLE (CALLED A HUMVEE)

COUGAR (BLAST-RESISTANT TROOP CARRIER)

WEAPONS
Tactical advantage
Night vision and thermal sighting (using heat to "see" in the dark) allow for attacks under cover of darkness.

TRANSPORT
Moving around
In the desert, vehicles must cope with rough tracks instead of roads, as well as hidden bombs. Control of airspace keeps the enemy from tracking troop movements on the ground.

73

MQ-1 SPY PLANE

Spies in the sky
Many inventions are first used by the military. New technology such as these unmanned, remote-controlled drones both large (above) and small (right) can spy on or target the enemy day or night.

High or low tech?
A future of high-tech weaponry is likely for many. But others will still rely on mass-produced but effective weapons such as the AK-47.

THE FUTURE SOLDIER?

FUTURE WARRIOR

The next generation of fighters will need to deal with an enemy that has high-tech information and weaponry. Future warriors may be equipped with stealth armor and lightweight assault rifles. They will have to adapt fast to changing conditions, but they still need to have one key quality: bravery.

Computer combat
Soldiers can already fight far from the front line by instructing unmanned aerial vehicles (UAVs) or drones to strike at the enemy.

Battlefield network
Smartphones help soldiers do more than just communicate. Military apps can pinpoint enemies, choose weapons, track drones, and even treat injuries.

TECHNOLOGY
New metamaterials
Future soldiers may wear clothes made of materials that bend light waves so that they will be harder to spot when they are in enemy territory.

Clear-sighted
This sight is raised when the soldier wants to use the underslung grenade launcher.

Picatinny rail
This can be fitted with day- or night-sighting systems.

Smart bullet
A recent breakthrough is the invention of a self-steering bullet, which can hit moving targets with extreme accuracy.

Adjustable buttstock
This can be adjusted to six different lengths to suit the soldier. It can also be folded in when not in use.

Underslung grenade launcher
This gives extra firepower. It can also be taken off to use separately.

Magazine
The release for this can be operated by either the left or the right hand.

FN SCAR MK 17 assault rifle
This CQC (close-quarter combat) rifle weighs only 7.7 pounds (3.5 kg). It has a range of 1,640 feet (500 m) and can be shortened for carrying.

Piston system
This contains the gases, keeping the rest of the rifle clean.

HK416 assault rifle
Used by the special forces of many different countries, this piston-driven automatic rifle can fire 850 rounds per minute. It is very reliable, whatever the conditions.

Torch
A beam of light helps target an enemy.

Drum magazine
This holds 50 rounds of ammunition.

WEAPONS
Multitask weaponry
Many of the latest weapons are laser guided and carry out more than one function. In the future, space-based lasers may be able to zap the enemy.

Fictional warrior
Robot warriors play central roles in many sci-fi movies, including the Terminator films, the latest of which is *Terminator Genisys*.

75

glossary

ambush
To attack from a hiding place. An ambush is a surprise attack.

amphibious
Trained to fight both on land and at sea.

artillery
Large military weapons that can fire missiles over long distances.

bayonet
A daggerlike weapon that can be attached to the barrel of a gun and used for stabbing or slashing.

blitzkrieg
A fast and intensive military attack. *Blitzkrieg* means "lightning war" in German.

boss
A metal stud on a shield that protects the hand of the warrior holding it.

broadsword
A large sword with a wide blade.

camouflage
The disguising of troops or weapons with paint, nets, or foliage so that enemies cannot see them against their surroundings.

carbine
A lightweight, short-barreled rifle used by cavalry.

catapult
A weapon, like a large slingshot, used to fire missiles over walls.

cavalry
The part of an army that fights on horseback.

civil war
A war between different groups within the same country.

clan
A group of people who are related by ancestry or marriage.

Corinthian
From the ancient Greek city of Corinth.

CQC
Used to fight at close range. *CQC* stands for *close-quarters combat*.

crossbow
A medieval weapon with a short bow mounted across a longer piece of wood.

culture
The ideas, beliefs, customs, and arts of a group of people or a country.

cure
To treat leather to soften it and keep it from decaying.

drone
An aircraft without a pilot that is controlled remotely.

flash grenade
A nonlethal grenade that makes a bright light to disorient enemies.

gladiator
A man in ancient Rome who fought other men or wild animals, often to the death, to provide entertainment.

grenade
A small bomb that explodes on contact when thrown by hand or fired.

guerrilla
A member of a small group of fighters that often launches surprise attacks against an official army.

Mace
Used during the Middle Ages, solid metal maces and war hammers could do great damage to a knight's armor.

hostage
Someone who is kept prisoner by a person or organization that demands something in return for the release of the captured person.

infantryman
A soldier who fights on foot.

javelin
A short, lightweight spear, usually thrown by hand.

joust
A competition between two knights on horseback with long spears or lances.

laser
A device that produces a narrow, intense beam of light. *Laser* stands for *Light Amplification by Stimulated Emission of Radiation*.

martial arts
The traditional, weaponless styles of self-defense and single combat practiced in Asia. Judo, karate, aikido, and kung fu are martial arts.

Mughal
Related to the Muslim dynasty that ruled much of India from the 16th to the 19th century.

musket
A long-barreled gun that is fired from the shoulder.

patriot
Someone who wholeheartedly supports and defends his or her country.

phalanx
An arrangement of ancient Greek infantry, formed in close ranks with shields joined and long spears overlapping.

pike
A long pole with a pointed metal tip, used as a weapon.

Prussian
From Prussia, a former state in northern Europe that was a military power in the 18th century.

redoubt
A structure made of earth, built as a fortification.

scabbard
A case that holds a sword or dagger.

siege
An operation carried out to capture a fortified town or castle by surrounding it, stopping all communications and supplies, and attacking it.

silencer
A device that is attached to the muzzle of a gun to reduce the sound of its firing.

slavery
The condition of being owned by another person and thought of as property.

sniper
A person who shoots at an enemy from a concealed place.

submachine gun
A lightweight automatic or semiautomatic gun that is fired from the shoulder or hip.

Templar
A knight of a religious military order founded by Crusaders in Jerusalem around 1118.

tomahawk
A lightweight ax used by North American Indians as a tool or weapon.

Valhalla
The hall of the Scandinavian god Odin, where the souls of Viking heroes slain in battle were said to go.

Halberd
A 17th-century Dutch foot soldier would have carried this two-handed weapon—an ax blade and spike mounted on a long wooden pole.

index

acknowledgments

123RF: 17 br soldier (Andrey Fadeev), 63 c tank (David Gilbert), 63 c jet (ivdwolf), 63 bc jeep (Robert Wilson), 16 fire bg, 17 fire bg (Roy Longmuir), 62 cr machine gun (snak), 9 tr maps, 11 tr maps, 17 tr maps, 21 tr maps, 24 cl maps, 27 tr maps, 31 tr maps, 37 tr maps, 39 tr maps, 42 cl maps, 45 tr maps, 51 tr maps, 57 tr maps, 60 cl maps, 63 tr maps (Teerawut Masawat), 8 tr helmet (trebuchet), 27 tl helmet (Volodymyr Krasyuk), 69 bl (Worradirek Muksab); Adams County Historical Society: 55 portrait; Alamy Images: 37 bc (AF archive), 27 bl (Arif Iqball Photography - Japan), 49 br soldier (Cernan Elias), 9 bl shield (Dorling Kindersley ltd), 75 bl (dpa picture alliance), 12, 13, 17 bc Thor, 44 bc (Heritage Image Partnership Ltd), 57 br soldier (Holmes Garden Photos), 31 br Inca (Kuttig - Travel), 44 l chief (Michele Burgess), 1 (Nelson Varghese), 42 cr portrait (Old Paper Studios), 45 br Boer (Photos 12), 75 br (Pictorial Press Ltd), 32 coins (PjrStudio), 35 flint dagger (Prisma Archivo), 38 c drum (Purestock), 45 tr portrait (Tim Gainey), 69 br soldiers (US Navy Photo), 63 cr portrait (World History Archive); AP Images: 60 cl, 62 bc (Bettmann), 63 bc (Eddie Adams), 62 l, 65 photo (Henri Huet), 62 br (Horst Faas); Art Resource, NY: 27 tr drawing (Ashmolean Museum), 46 t pistol, 66 l, 67 cr helmet (The Metropolitan Museum of Art); Bapty/Gary Ombler: 6 armor, 7 vest, 8 t spear, 9 c swords, 14 sword, 18 r shield, 27 tr pattern, 59 tr pattern, all other uncredited objects throughout cover and book; Bigstock/Mapman: 38 cr musket ball; BNPS/www.bnps.co.uk: 44 r shield; Bridgeman Art Library: 24 cl painting (Bibliotheque Nationale, Paris), 28, 29 (Maidstone Museum and Art Gallery, Kent, UK), 37 c (Peter Newark Military Pictures); Caroline Nicolay: 11 br soldier; Corbis Images: 63 r guerilla (Bettmann), 48 l warrior (Dave G. Houser), 9 tl armor (Leemage); DARPA: 75 tr; Defense Imagery: 63 tr portrait; Dreamstime: 74 bc (Alessio Tricani), 37 tr statue (Alexandre Fagundes De Fagundes), 16 bc chip (Algol), 8 bc armor, 8 c helmet (Angellodeco), 26 l samurai, 36 bc (Attila Jandi), 69 br bg (Chad Anderson), 38 l bg (Christian Delbert), 9 cr vase (Dtopal), 54 book, 55 book (Dvmsimages), 67 tc helmet (Emil Djumailiev), 73 tr helicopter (Falcon47), 20 bc swords (Franxyz), 68 bc (Iaroslav Horbunov), 26 bc (Jose Gil), 39 bl (Kathleen Handy), 49 tr pattern (Ken Backer), 27 br bg (Kitano), 31 br bg (Kseniya Ragozina), 21 bl (Mariusz Prusaczyk), cover main (Nattapon Tabtong), 21 br knight (Nejron), 68 c grenade (Nerthuz), 16 tr figurehead (Oleg Doroshin), 72 l (Oleg Zabielin), 26 l bg (Qweszxcj), 73 br (Robert Sholl), 56 tr medal (Rotarepok), 16 br, 17 bl (Sebastiang), 38 bc (Sergey Rogovets), 59 br soldier (Sergeyussr), 74 l bg (Vasily Smirnov), 10 bl soldiers (Verity Johnson), 21 br bg (Victor Soares), 9 br (Vladimir Korostyshevskiy), 64 folder, 65 folder (Vlntn), 9 bc (Yiannis Papadimitriou); DVIDS: 74 t photo, 74 cl photo, 74 cr photo; Fotolia: 30 bc (McCarthys_PhotoWorks), 31 tr pattern (trotsky1905); Getty Images: 24 c portrait (Archive Photos), 8 l warrior (Cristian Baitg), 18 l shield (DEA Picture Library), 24 tc portrait (Guildhall Library & Art Gallery/ Heritage Images), 36 l musketeer (Jacques Lange/Paris Match), 58 br, 58 bc (Keystone-France), 58 bg, 59 bg (MPI), 58 l soldier (Popperfoto), 57 tr portrait (Universal History Archive/UIG); Imperial War Museum, Photograph Archive: 58 cl (Mapham J (Sgt)), 58 cr (Spender (Lt)), 56 l, 56 bc; iStockphoto: 22 pages, 23 pages (2happy), 27 br ninja (4x6), 63 tr pattern (Achim Prill), 36 l bg (Alfonso Cacciola), 22 book border, 23 book border (ariusz), 73 tc grenade (belterz), 63 c helicopter (breckeni), 44 bg, 45 bg (Brian Raisbeck), 11 tr pattern, 14 t pattern, 15 t pattern (Chunhai Cao), 15 br (CSA-Archive), 73 cr plane (CT757fan), 32 coins, 33 coins (curtoicurto), 45 br bg (DavidCallan), 54 photo frame (Dawn Mayfarth), 22 quill (DNY59), 11 cl army (doubtfulneddy), 2 l fg, 3 l fg, 21 tr pattern (duncan1890), 37 tl hat (Easy_Asa), 10 bc sword (eyecrave), 42 compass (FrankCangelosi), 10 l bg (Fyletto), 67 br helmet (GBlakeley), 37 tr pattern (gbrundin), 73 tr portrait (GeorgiosArt), 68 l bg (gong hangxu), 59 br bg (H20addict), 57 br bg (Havana1234), 39 c drawing (HultonArchive), 24 bg, 25 bg, 42 bg, 43 bg, 60 bg, 61 bg (imagedepotpro), 44 l bg (Jeremy Richards), 20 l knight (JochenK), 33 coins (Joe Cicak), 39 tr soldier (joeygil), 3 r fg (Johncairns), 39 bc (Johnrob), revolver cylinder throughout (jrsower), 74 bg, 75 bg (kokoroyuki), 30 l bg (KostyaK), 48 l bg (Kubrak78), 22 crest, 23 crest (ly86), 51 tr pattern (Maher), 54 border bg, 55 border bg (MaksimMazur), 45 tr pattern (ManoAfrica), 20 l bg (matejmm), 49 br bg (Meinzahn), back cover bullet holes, 2 bullet holes, 3 bullet holes (Miroslav Boskov), cover bg, back cover bg, 2 bg, 3 bg, 6 bg, 7 bg (mysondanube), 30 bg, 31 bg (naisupakit), 64 card (Nic_Taylor), 38 bg, 39 bg (NormaZaro), 4 bg, 5 bg, 78 bg, 79 bg (ozgurdonmaz), 11 tr statue (PaoloGaetano), 10 bg marble, 11 bg marble (phatthanit_r), 64 paper clip, 65 paper clip (pixhook), back cover bc helmet, 66 r, 67 l (Plainview), 36 flag bg, 37 flag bg (Ramberg), 14 scroll, 15 scroll (ranplett), 9 tr pattern (RapidEye), 21 tr portrait (RFStock), 16 c ship (rimglow), 17 br bg (rjmiz), 73 cr Humvee, 73 cr cougar (Rockfinder), 73 tr pattern (Sami Sert), 56 bg, 57 bg (sbayram), 60 compass (Serafima82), 10 l soldier (Spanic), 32 book, 33 book (sqback), 63 r bg (szefei), 64 border bg, 65 border bg (tarczas), 24 compass (tharrison), 11 br bg (tirc83), 64 papers, 65 papers (tomograf), 31 tr drawing (traveler1116), 22 border bg, 23 border bg, 32 border bg, 33 border bg (ulkan), 69 tr pattern (Vaara), 10 c catapult (will_iredale), 8 l bg (WitR), 14 stone bg, 15 stone bg (wuttichok), 57 tr pattern (zhudifeng); Ken Bohrer/Americanrevolutionphotos.com: 38 l soldier, 39 br soldier, 40, 41; Library of Congress: 50 l bg, 52, 53, 80 (Andrew J. Russell), 51 br soldier (Charles R. Rees), 48 bg, 48 bc, 49 bg (Edward S. Curtis Collection), 51 tr portrait (Frederick Gutekunst), 51 br bg (George N. Barnard), 4 bc (Gift of Tom Liljenquist 2010 (DLC/PP-2010:105)), 50 l soldier (Gift of Tom Liljenquist 2011 (DLC/PP-2012:127)), 50 c photo (Gift of Tom Liljenquist 2012 (DLC/PP-2012:127)), 51 tc portrait (Julian Vannerson), 42 ct portrait (London & Carlisle, Printed for R. Faulder, bookseller, [etc.], 1780, v. 1, p. 204.), 50 br (Mathew B. Brady), 50 bc, 54 photo (Timothy H. O'Sullivan), 2 r fg, 39 tr banner, 42 cl drawing, 49 tr portrait, 55 photo frame; Martyn Chillmaid: 17 bl figure; Michelle Middleton: 16 l Viking, 78 silhouette; Navy.mil/SEAL + SWCC: 70; Science Source/Alfred Pasieka: 74 tl drone; Shutterstock, Inc.: 51 c cannon (4736202690), 9 cr relief (Anastasios71), 17 tr pattern (Asmus), 17 tr portrait (Denise Kappa), back cover br robot, 74 l robot (DM7), 59 tr portrait (Elzbieta Sekowska), 30 l conquistador (Klter), 67 bc helmet (Olemac), 26 br (Radu Razvan), 38 br (Tim Pleasant), 68 l soldier (Vudhikrai), 58 l bg (YellowPaul); Thinkstock/Peter Spiro: 39 br bg; Tim Loughhead/Precision Illustration: 16 cb artwork, 24 battle map, 25 battle map, 31 cr club, 42 battle map, 43 battle map, 60 battle map, 61 battle map; US Army: 73 bl (Spc. Scott Davis), 72 bc (Spc. Tia Sokimson), 79 silhouette; Wikimedia: 24 flags, 42 flags, 60 flags.

Special thanks to all the staff at Bapty, but particularly Tony Watts and his family; Tim Loughhead for the battle artwork; Clare Joyce for the mapwork; and Ken Bohrer and Caroline Nicolay for the supply of extra images.

War zone
This scene of devastation from the American Civil War has been echoed through history as warriors have fought for their countries.